CRITICAL THINKING
FOR SOCIAL WORKERS

Adventures in Social Research: Data Analysis Using SPSS by Earl Babbie and Fred Halley

Adventures in Social Research: Data Analysis Using SPSS for WINDOWS by Earl Babbie and Fred Halley

Critical Thinking for Social Workers: A Workbook by Leonard Gibbs and Eileen Gambrill

Race, Ethnicity, Gender, and Class: The Sociology of Group Conflict and Change by Joseph F. Healey

The Production of Reality: Essays and Readings in Social Psychology by Peter Kollock and Jodi O'Brien

Aging: Concepts and Controversies by Harry R. Moody, Jr.

Diversity in America by Vincent N. Parrillo

The McDonaldization of Society, Revised Ed., by George Ritzer

Expressing America: A Critique of the Global Credit Card Society by George Ritzer

Shifts in the Social Contract: Understanding Change in American Society by Beth Rubin

Worlds of Difference: Structured Inequality and the Aging Experience by Eleanor Palo Stoller and Rose Campbell Gibson

The Pine Forge Press Series in Research Methods and Statistics
Edited by Richard T. Campbell and Kathleen S. Crittenden

Investigating the Social World: The Process and Practice of Research by Russell K. Schutt

A Guide to Field Research by Carol A. Bailey

Designing Surveys: A Guide to Decisions and Procedures by Ronald Czaja and Johnny Blair

How Sampling Works by Caroline Hodges Persell and Richard Maisel

Sociology for a New Century
A Pine Forge Press Series edited by Charles Ragin, Wendy Griswold, and Larry Griffin

How Societies Change by Daniel Chirot

Cultures and Societies in a Changing World by Wendy Griswold

Crime and Disrepute by John Hagan

Gods in the Global Village by Lester R. Kurtz

Constructing Social Research by Charles C. Ragin

Women and Men at Work by Barbara Reskin and Irene Padavic

Cities in a World Economy by Saskia Sassen

CRITICAL THINKING
FOR SOCIAL WORKERS
A Workbook

LEONARD GIBBS

Department of Social Work
University of Wisconsin, Eau Claire

EILEEN GAMBRILL

School of Social Welfare
University of California, Berkeley

Pine Forge Press
Thousand Oaks, California • London • New Delhi

To Betsy, Martin, and Jeff—L. G.

*With thanks and debts of gratitude to Gail and to the memory
of my parents, William and Irene Gambrill—E. G.*

For information, address:

 Pine Forge Press
A Sage Publications Company
2455 Teller Road
Thousand Oaks, California 91320
(805) 499-4224
E-mail: sales@pfp.sagepub.com

SAGE Publications Ltd.
6 Bonhill Street
London EC2A 4PU
United Kingdom

SAGE Publications India Pvt. Ltd.
M-32 Market
Greater Kailash I
New Delhi 110 048 India

Production Manager: Rebecca Holland
Production: Greg Hubit Bookworks
Design: Susan Benoit
Cover Design: Deborah Davis

*Grateful acknowledgment is made to Cyndee Kaiser
for the drawings throughout the book.*

For permission to reprint quotes, we also acknowledge:

From "Local Lady Took Natex Year Ago," Copyright May 27,
1935 The Morning Call, Inc., Allentown PA. Reprinted with
permission of The Morning Call.

From "India's Wolf Children," by R. M. Zingg (1941), Scientific
American, Volume 164(3). Copyright Scientific American.

Printed in the United States of America

96 97 98 99 10 9 8 7 6 5 4 3 2

ISBN: 0-8039-9050-2

About The Authors

Leonard Gibbs (MSSW, ACSW) received his Ph.D. at the University of Wisconsin at Madison in Social Welfare in 1977. He has since taught a full range of courses in the baccalaureate program in social work at the University of Wisconsin at Eau Claire. Much of his research has concerned teaching and ways to improve practice decision-making. He is the author of the textbook, *Scientific Reasoning for Social Workers*.

Eileen Gambrill is a Professor in the School of Social Welfare at the University of California at Berkeley. She has been interested in the area of critical thinking for many years and has given workshops on critical thinking for professionals in the United States, Ireland, and England. Recent publications include *Critical Thinking in Clinical Practice, Controversial Issues in Social Work* (with Robert Pruger), *Controversial Issues in Child Welfare* (with T. J. Stein), and *Debating Children's Lives: Current Controversies on Children and Adolescents* (with Mary Ann Mason).

About The Publisher

Pine Forge Press is a new educational publisher, dedicated to publishing innovative books and software throughout the social sciences. On this and any other of our publications, we welcome your comments and suggestions.

Please call or write to:

Pine Forge Press
A Sage Publications Company
2455 Teller Road
Thousand Oaks, California 91320

(805) 499-4224

FAX (805) 499-7881

E-mail: sales@pfp.sagepub.com

BRIEF CONTENTS

DETAILED CONTENTS

The Introduction defines critical thinking, describes how it relates to scientific thinking, and identifies related knowledge, skills, values, and attitudes. The purpose of critical thinking is to help professionals make well-reasoned judgments and take actions that benefit clients. The costs and benefits of critical thinking are discussed.

Professionals differ in the criteria they use to select assessment, intervention, and evaluation methods. This exercise directs readers to compare the criteria they use to make decisions about recommended intervention methods in different contexts.

This exercise offers readers an opportunity to review their beliefs about knowledge (what it is and how to get it). Presented are common misconceptions and misunderstandings that may interfere with offering clients the benefits of available knowledge.

Professionals and laypeople alike hear many claims about how to help people. In this exercise students watch a videotaped advertisement (Part A of the video-tape included with the Instructors' Manual) and complete a questionnaire. This exercise identifies earmarks of human-service advertisements and raises questions about relying on them as a guide to making decisions.

PREFACE

This workbook has a single purpose: *that those who do its exercises will reason more effectively about life-affecting practice decisions.* Critical thinking involves the critical appraisal of beliefs, arguments, and claims in order to arrive at well-reasoned judgments. Critical thinking is essential to helping people because it encourages practitioners to evaluate the soundness of beliefs, arguments, and claims. *What helpers believe influences what they do!* Thus, it is important to examine beliefs in relation to their accuracy. Will sending a youthful offender to boot camp be more effective in decreasing future offenses than placing him on probation? Will group treatment for a wife batterer be more effective than individual treatment? Which methods will most likely increase the participation of community residents working with citizens' boards? Social workers make many such judgments and decisions daily. Deciding which actions will help clients is an inescapable part of being a professional. Thinking critically about claims, beliefs, and arguments can help professionals arrive at beliefs and actions that are well reasoned.

Thinking critically is important for all areas of social work, including practice, research, social policy, and administration. Critical-thinking skills will help you to spot policies and procedures that benefit agencies but not their clients and those that maintain discriminatory patterns of service. These skills and related values and attitudes, such as being open minded and flexible as well as self-critical, will encourage recognition of and respect for cultural differences.

This workbook is designed to learn by doing. A workbook requires action as well as thinking. It involves readers actively in exercises related to making practice decisions at the individual, family, group, community, and societal level and allows for immediate feedback about decisions made. Think as much as you like, you cannot assess the effects of your thinking until you act. For instance, did your thinking result in decisions that benefit clients? Not only may a workbook foster better learning, it makes learning enjoyable. You are more likely to continue learning tasks that are fun. Toward this aim, we have tried to create exercises that are enjoyable as well as instructive.

Many of the exercises involve cooperative learning. In spite of the literature in education supporting the benefits and enjoyment of cooperative (shared) learning among peers, social-work education has been "slow on the uptake." Here, you will be involved with your peers and/or colleagues in learning adventures designed to hone your critical-thinking skills. The exercises included are designed to be useful for all social work curricula. Some have been pretested, others are new. Each exercise includes the following sections: *Purpose, Background, Instructions,* and *Follow-up Question(s).*

The workbook exercises are designed to show that the knowledge and skills involved in research and practice overlap as decisions are made in everyday practice. Lack of integration between practice-related research and practice is a problem in all professions, including social work. Too often, professionals do not take advantage of practice-related research in making decisions that affect their clients. Because of this, clients may receive ineffective or harmful "help." One reason for this lack of integration lies in the very structure of professional curricula. Research courses are taught separately from practice courses, encouraging the false impression that research and practice are quite different enterprises. This dichotomy gets in the way of understanding the shared values, attitudes, content knowledge, and performance skills of research and practice. Critical discussion, whether with yourself or others, is integral to both. Research and practice are complementary, not competing areas.

Part 1, Critical Thinking, defines critical thinking, discusses why it especially matters in the helping professions, and describes related values, attitudes, knowledge, and skills. This part also contains two exercises. The first provides an opportunity to review the criteria you use to make decisions. In the next exercise, you assess your beliefs about knowledge (what it is and how to get it).

The three exercises in Part 2, Recognizing Propaganda in Human Services Advertising, demonstrate the importance of questioning claims that a method helps clients. Videotaped presentations of a human-services advertisement, a recorded speaker, and a treatment-program promotion portray vivid emotional appeals to convince viewers that a method works.

The six exercises in Part 3, Fallacies and Pitfalls in Professional Decision Making, are designed to help you to identify and remedy common fallacies and pitfalls in reasoning about practice. They rely on vignettes that illustrate situations that arise in everyday practice. Exercise 6 contains twenty-five vignettes that can be used to assess practice reasoning. The Reasoning-in-Practice Games (Exercises 7–9) involve working with other students to identify practice fallacies. In the Fallacies Film Festival, students work together to prepare a skit to demonstrate a fallacy. Example skits are included in Part C of the videotape that accompanies the Instructors' Manual. Exercise 11 provides an opportunity to spot fallacies in professional contexts (including your classroom experiences).

Part 4, Thinking Critically About Specific Assessment and Intervention Decisions, contains nine exercises. They include an exercise that encourages considering the effects of vague problem description. Other exercises encourage thinking critically about making predictions, selecting diagnostic tests and intervention methods, and preparing and reviewing case records. Exercise 12 provides a form that provides a template for reviewing the quality of practice-related research as well as the strength of a treatment's effect size (a numerical index that quantifies the magnitude of a treatment's effect). Exercise 15 provides an opportunity to think critically about practice-related ethical issues. Exercise 16 presents a case example of how practice reasoning can go wrong and some of the reasons why. Exercise 19 provides guidelines for reviewing the quality of arguments.

Part 5, Reviewing Educational and Practice Environments, includes two exercises. Exercise 21 provides a checklist for reviewing the extent to which an educational or work environment demonstrates a culture of thoughtfulness. Exercise 22 includes a rating form for evaluating how much instructors encourage critical thinking in their classrooms.

If working through the exercises contained in the workbook results in better services for clients, all our efforts, both yours and ours, will be worthwhile. We welcome your feedback about each exercise. In the spirit of critical thinking, we welcome negative as well as positive comments, especially those that offer concrete suggestions for improving exercises. Please write to us in care of Pine Forge Press (address is on page v). We hope that you enjoy and learn from participating in the exercises in this book.

LEONARD GIBBS   EILEEN GAMBRILL
lgibbs@uwec.edu   gambrill@uclink2.berkeley.edu

Note to Instructors: With the adoption of this book you will receive an Instructor's Manual and the videotape. The Instructor's Manual contains descriptions of each exercise in the Workbook, including a brief overview, the purpose, or learning objectives, of the exercise, the materials and time required, suggestions for using the exercise, and possible answers to the Follow-up Questions. The videotape includes a short example of a human-services advertisement advocating a treatment program, a famous Doctor Fox lecture that demonstrates the effect of style versus content on a lecture, a humorous Fallacies Film Festival made up of students' preposterous practice fallacy vignettes, and a role-played interview with a "depressed" person that demonstrates inter-rater reliability in assessment.

ACKNOWLEDGMENTS

We owe a great deal to kindred spirits both past and present who have highlighted the importance of practice decisions and helped us to learn how to think critically about them. All value (or did value) critical evaluation of claims of effectiveness in order to protect clients from ineffective or harmful services. A special note of thanks is extended to Sharon Ikami for her infinite patience, consistent good will, and superb typing skills and for serving as video specialist in preparing one of the sections on the videotape that accompanies the Instructors' Manual. We would also like to thank Loretta Morales (role-played interview in Part D of the videotape), Kathy Finder, Nancy Erickson, Kathryn Colbert (computer consultants), Monica Bares (typing and editorial help), Aaron Harder (video editing), Cyndee Kaiser (cartoons), Connie Kees (videotaping), Donald Naftulin (Dr. Fox lecture), Michael Hakeem (suggestions for some of the counterarguments in Exercise 2), Jim Ziegert, Mary Ann King (vignette for Reasoning-in-Practice Game C), Carol Williams, Brenda Peterson DeSousa, Lisa Roepke, Lisa Furst, Amy Simpson, Jennifer Neyes, Melissa Brown, Jennifer Mortt, Marcia Cigler, Beth Rusch, Carol Weis, Vicki Millard, Kristen Jensen, Mindy Olson, Laurie Buckler, Michelle LeCloux, Jennifer Owen, Tiffany Winrich, Pam McKee, Kelly Meyer, Reggie Bicha, Tara Lehman, Julie Garvey, Richard Lockwood, Kate Kremer, Cory Heckel, Mike Werner, Jill Eslinger (Fallacies Film Festival vignettes), Margie Anderson (permission to use Rogers Hospital video), Macmillan Publishers (permission to use the Professional Thinking Form and Quality of Study Rating Form), and Grafton Hull (content areas in suggested uses for our exercises in Five Social Work Curriculum Areas, Exhibit P.1).

Leonard Gibbs would especially like to acknowledge the influence of a great teacher, Professor Emeritus Michael Hakeem of the University of Wisconsin at Madison. We also want to thank Steve Rutter of Pine Forge Press for his enthusiasm, shared vision, and support. And, finally, we wish to acknowledge the encouragement and financial support of the University of Wisconsin at Eau Claire Foundation and the College of Professional Studies, whose support was essential to this work, as well as the Committee on Research, the University of California at Berkeley.

Exhibit P.1   Suggested Uses for Exercises in Five Social Work Curriculum Areas

Exercise Number (#); Abbrev. Title	Human Behavior and the Social Environment	Social Welfare Policies/Programs; Introductory Classes	Research	Practice	Ethics
#1 Making Decisions		Explore implications of self-interest versus common good	Highlight relevance of research to life-affecting decisions	Highlight relevance of research to life-affecting decisions	Highlight ethical issues related to practice decisions
#2 Beliefs About Knowledge	Highlight how beliefs about knowledge influence assumptions about what can be discovered about behavior	Highlight how beliefs about knowledge influence selection of policies	Study philosophy of science as it relates to research	Review relevance of personal beliefs about knowledge to practice decisions	Explore relevance of beliefs about knowledge to making ethical decisions
#3 Human-Service Advertisements	Review hidden assumptions about behavior in advertisements	Emphasize the importance of critically evaluating policies and programs	Show relevance of research-related questions to evaluating practice claims	Encourage critical analysis of claims that practice methods work	Raise questions about ethics of persuasion
#4 Doctor Fox	Encourage helpers to critically evaluate claims about behavior	Illustrate the potential influence of political rhetoric	Enhance motivation to focus on data, not style	Encourage practitioners to be wary of practice gurus	Raise questions about whether it is ethical to persuade people with your style
#5 Scaring Youth to "Go Straight"	Illustrate assumptions about behavior and their influence on practice decisions	Illustrate an intervention program that spreads with no data and harmful effects	Evaluate scientific reasoning skills	Evaluate vulnerability to propaganda	Raise ethical questions about use of propagandistic promotional presentations
#6 Professional Thinking Form	Illustrate assumptions about behavior and their influence on practice decisions	Evaluate critical thinking in introductory course	Discuss or evaluate scientific reasoning skills	Discuss or evaluate reasoning about practice for better decision making	Discuss ethical issues related to practice decisions

Exercise Number (#); Abbrev. Title	Human Behavior and the Social Environment	Social Welfare Policies/Programs; Introductory Classes	Research	Practice	Ethics
Exhibit P.1 (continued)		Suggested Uses for Exercises in Five Social Work Curriculum Areas			
#7 Game A: Common Practice Fallacies	Illustrate assumptions about behavior and how they affect practice	Use in introductory classes to foster critical thinking	Help transfer scientific reasoning to practice	Foster critical discussion about practice decisions	Use vignettes for discussion in Exercise 15
#8 Game B: Group and Interpersonal Dynamics	Illustrate group processes	Demonstrate how political meetings can lack effec- tiveness	Illustrate how group pressure and groupthink can defeat logic	Enhance skills in resisting groupthink	Use vignettes for discussion in Exercise 15
#9 Game C: Cognitive Biases	Illustrate influ- ence of cognitive variables on inferences made about behavior	Highlight sources of error in making policy decisions	Demonstrate usefulness of research related to clinical reasoning	Demonstrate sources of error that may affect practice decisions	Use vignettes for discussion in Exercise 15
#10 Fallacies Film Festival	Practice spotting questionable assumptions about behavior	Inform and delight intro- ductory students with fallacies films made by advanced students	Provide an opportunity for students to transfer scien- tific reasoning to practice situations	Show humor- ously how poor practice reason- ing can affect service	Highlight ethi- cal implications of questionable practice decisions
#11 Fallacy Spotting in Professional Contexts	Spot fallacies in popular beliefs about people	Spot fallacies in policy literature	Spot fallacies in research literature	Spot fallacies in practice literature	Consider ethical implications of fallacies
#12 Evaluating Study Quality	Evaluate research related to human development	Critically review research related to policy decisions	Highlight criteria impor- tant to consider in evaluating research	Highlight crite- ria important to consider when reviewing practice-related research	Highlight ethi- cal issues related to care- fully evaluating practice-related research

Exercise Number (#); Abbrev. Title	Human Behavior and the Social Environment	Social Welfare Policies/Programs; Introductory Classes	Research	Practice	Ethics
#13 Describing Problems in Assessment	Highlight the importance of clearly describing behavior	Highlight the importance of clearly describing behavior	Discuss reliability and validity	Emphasize the relevance of validity and reliability to practice decisions	Raise ethical concerns related to reliance on vague descriptions
#14 Making Predictions	Highlight difficulties in making predictions about what people will do	Highlight difficulties in making predictions about what people will do	Demonstrate principles of decision analysis	Demonstrate how to assess risk	Raise ethical issues about clinical vs. statistical prediction
#15 Critical Thinking As an Ethical Guide		Examine ethical issues related to policy making	Examine ethical issues in research	Examine ethical issues in practice	Examine variety of ethical issues in practice
#16 Error As Process	Illustrate problems of making judgments about people	Demonstrate sources of bias	Demonstrate sources of bias	Demonstrate sources of error in making practice decisions	Highlight ethical implications of poor reasoning
#17 Evaluating Diagnostic Tests	Highlight problems of relying on diagnostic tests when making inferences about behavior	Highlight problems of relying on diagnostic tests when making inferences about behavior	Highlight the importance of using valid, reliable measures	Highlight the importance of using valid, reliable measures	Highlight ethical questions that should be raised about diagnostic tests
#18 Reviewing Intervention Plans		Illustrate relevance of research to policy decisions	Illustrate relevance of research to practice decisions	Highlight criteria for reviewing intervention plans	Highlight ethical questions related to selection of plans

Exercise Number (#); Abbrev. Title	Human Behavior and the Social Environment	Social Welfare Policies/Programs; Introductory Classes	Research	Practice	Ethics
#19 Analyzing Arguments	Enhance skills in critically evaluating arguments related to behavior	Enhance skills in critically evaluating arguments related to policy decisions	Enhance skills in critically evaluating arguments found in research literature	Enhance skills in critically evaluating arguments related to practice decisions	Enhance skills in critically evaluating arguments from an ethical perspective
#20 Thinking Critically About Case Records	Highlight problems related to using written records to understand behavior	Highlight questions that should be raised about written documents related to policy decisions	Highlight questions that should be raised about use of written documents in research	Integrate critical thinking concepts into record keeping	Highlight ethical questions related to inaccurate or incomplete records
#21 Encouraging a Culture of Thoughtfulness	Evaluate the culture of an organization	Evaluate climate within which policy decisions are made	Highlight importance of critical discussion in research	Evaluate workplace climate as this influences practice decisions	Emphasize the relevance of critical discussion to quality of service
#22 Evaluating the Teaching of Critical Thinking	Evaluate instruction	Evaluate instruction	Evaluate instruction	Evaluate instruction	Highlight ethical implications of critical discussion

Exhibit P.1 (continued)   *Suggested Uses for Exercises in Five Social Work Curriculum Areas*

1 CRITICAL THINKING
What it is and why it is important

Introduction

THE ROLE OF CRITICAL THINKING IN THE HELPING PROFESSIONS

Consider the following scenarios. A professor tells you: "Some people who have a problem with alcohol can learn to be controlled drinkers; abstinence is not required for all people." Will you believe her simply because she says so? If not, what information will you seek and why? How will you evaluate the data you collect?

Your supervisor says, "Refer the client to the Altona Family Service Agency. They know how to help these clients." Will you take her advice? What questions will help you decide?

A case record you are reading states, "Mrs. Lynch abuses her child because she is schizophrenic. She has been diagnosed as schizophrenic by two psychiatrists. Thus, there is little that can be done to improve her parenting skills." What questions will you ask? Why?

An advertisement for a residential treatment center for youth claims, "We've been serving youth for over fifty years with success." Does this convince you? If not, what kind of evidence will you seek and why?

You read an article stating that "grass-roots community organization will not be effective in alienated neighborhoods." What questions would you raise?

Finally, a social worker tells you that because Mrs. Smith recalls having been abused as a child, and because she has been through counseling before, insight therapy will be the most effective course to help her overcome her related depression and anger. Do you believe him?

If you thought carefully about these statements, you engaged in critical thinking. Critical thinking involves the careful examination and evaluation of beliefs and actions. It requires paying attention to the process of reasoning, not just the product. In this broad definition, critical thinking is much more than the appraisal of claims and arguments, more than a set of tools for discovering mistakes in thinking. Well-reasoned thinking is a form of creation and construction. Reasoning has a purpose.

Paul (1993) lists purpose first as one component of critical thinking (see Exhibit 1). What is the purpose of thinking about practice-related questions? If our purpose is to help clients, then we must carefully consider our beliefs and actions. Critical thinking involves the use of standards such as clarity, accuracy, relevance, and completeness. It requires evaluating evidence, considering alternative points of view, and being genuinely fair-minded in accurately presenting opposing views. Critical thinkers make a genuine effort to critique fairly all views, preferred and unpreferred. They value accuracy over "winning" or social approval. Questions that arise when you think critically include:

1. How do I know a claim is true?
2. Who said the claim was accurate? What could their motives be? How reliable are these sources?
3. Are the presented facts correct?
4. Have any facts been omitted?
5. Have there been any critical tests of this claim? Have any experimental studies been done? Were these studies relatively

---

Exhibit 1

Characteristics of Critical Thinking

1. It is purposeful.
2. It is responsive to and guided by *intellectual standards* (relevance, accuracy, precision, clarity, depth, and breadth).
3. It supports the development of intellectual *traits* in the thinker of humility, integrity, perseverance, empathy, and self-discipline.
4. The thinker can identify the *elements of thought* present in thinking about any problem, such that the thinker makes the logical connection between the elements and the problem at hand. The critical thinker will routinely ask the following questions:

   - What is the *purpose* of my thinking (goal/objective)?
   - What precise *question* (problem) am I trying to answer?
   - Within what *point of view* (perspective) am I thinking?
   - What *concepts* or ideas are central to my thinking?
   - What am I taking for granted, what *assumptions* am I making?
   - What *information* am I using (data, facts, observation)?
   - How am I *interpreting* that information?
   - What *conclusions* am I coming to?
   - If I accept the conclusions, what are the *implications?* What would the consequence be if I put my thoughts into action?

   For each element, the thinker must consider standards that shed light on the effectiveness of her thinking.

5. It is *self-assessing and self-improving.* The thinker takes steps to assess her thinking, using appropriate intellectual standards. If you are not assessing your thinking, you are not thinking critically.
6. *There is an integrity to the whole system.* The thinker is able to critically examine her thought as a whole and to take it apart (consider its parts as well). The thinker is committed to be intellectually humble, persevering, courageous, fair, and just. The critical thinker is aware of the variety of ways in which thinking can become distorted, misleading, prejudiced, superficial, unfair, or otherwise defective.
7. It *yields a well-reasoned answer.* If we know how to check our thinking and are committed to doing so, and we get extensive practice, then we can depend on the results of our thinking being productive.
8. It is responsive to the social and moral imperative to enthusiastically argue from opposing points of view and to *seek and identify weakness and limitations in one's own position.* Critical thinkers are aware that there are many legitimate points of view, each of which (when deeply thought through) may yield some level of insight.

Source: R. Paul (1993, pp. 20–23).

---

free of bias? Have their results been replicated? What samples were used? How representative were they? Was random assignment used?

6. Are there other plausible explanations?
7. If correlations are presented, how strong are they?
8. What weak appeals are used (e.g., to emotion or special interests)?

"Specialized knowledge may be required to think effectively in any domain; in general, the more one knows the better" (Nickerson, 1988, p. 13). Creativity also plays a role in critical thinking. For instance, creativity is required to discover assumptions, alternative explanations, and biases. Thinking styles, attitudes, and strategies associated with creativity are

- readiness to explore and to change
- attention to problem finding as well as problem solving
- immersion in a task
- restructuring of understanding
- belief that knowing and understanding are products of one's intellectual process
- withholding of judgment
- emphasis on understanding
- thinking in terms of opposites
- valuing complexity, ambiguity, and uncertainty combined with an interest in finding order
- valuing feedback but not deferring to convention and social pressures
- recognizing multiple perspectives on a topic
- deferring closure in the early stages of a creative task (based on Greeno, 1989; Nickerson, Perkins, & Smith, 1985; Weisberg, 1986).

THE IMPORTANCE OF CRITICAL THINKING

Does critical thinking matter? Are clients likely to receive better services if social workers use critical-thinking skills? Research, both historical and empirical, shows that it does matter. The history of the helping professions demonstrates that caring is not enough to protect people from harmful practices and to insure that they receive helpful services (Breggin, 1991; Morgan, 1983; Szasz, 1994). These are some of the errors that may occur if incomplete or inaccurate perspectives are accepted:

- Misclassifying clients
- Continuing intervention too long
- Focusing on irrelevant factors
- Selecting weak intervention methods (e.g., offering psychological counseling when clients need material resources)
- Increasing client dependency
- Overlooking client assets
- Describing behavior unrelated to its context
- Withdrawing intervention too soon
- Not arranging for the generalization and maintenance of positive gains

The danger of thinking uncritically is that time and resources may be wasted—or worse, that clients won't get the help they need. Examples of ineffective intervention and iatrogenic effects (helper-induced harm) include institutionalizing healthy deaf children because they were incorrectly labeled as having emotional problems (Lane, 1991), institutionalizing adolescents for treatment of substance abuse even though there is no evidence that this works (Schwartz, 1989), and negligent medical care in American hospitals that injures or kills approximately 100,000 people annually (Health Letter, 1992, p. 1). When ineffective methods fail, clients may feel more hopeless and helpless than ever about achieving desired outcomes (Mays & Franks, 1985). Methods may be selected because of how entertainingly they are described, not their effectiveness. Some interventions may be offered because they are easiest to administer or because they earn money for the provider. Ineffective or harmful methods may be chosen because of faulty reasoning on the part of practitioners. Fortunately, you can learn skills that will help you make sound decisions.

WHAT CRITICAL THINKING OFFERS

Critical thinking will help you make wise choices—to select those options that, compared with others, are most likely to help clients attain the outcomes they value. It will also help you evaluate claims and arguments so you can recognize bogus claims that may get in the way of helping clients.

EVALUATE THE ACCURACY OF CLAIMS

Social workers are deluged by claims and arguments such as the following: "Use genograms; they can help you to help your clients." "Use behavioral methods; they work." "Don't use school-based sexual-molestation prevention programs. They don't work." Such claims may or may not be accompanied by clear arguments. People use many kinds of criteria to evaluate these claims. For instance, you can assess the accuracy of a claim in relation to predictions that have been tested. Or you can use quite different criteria, such as anecdotal experience or the manner of a speaker's presentation. False or questionable claims are often accepted because they are not carefully evaluated.

EVALUATE ARGUMENTS

Making decisions involves suggesting arguments in favor of pursuing one course of action rather than another; of believing one claim rather than another. (See Exhibit 2). In an argument, some statements (the premises) support or provide evidence for another statement (the conclusion). The goal of an argument is to *investigate* the truth or falsity of a particular claim. A key part of an argument is the claim, conclusion, or position that is put forward. A second key part comprises the reasons or premises offered to support the claim. A third consists of the reasons given for assuming that the premises are relevant to the conclusion. These are called warrants. Here's an example of an argument not supported by its warrant:

- Premise: Ritalin [a brand of methylphenidate] decreases hyperactivity among children so their academic performance can improve.

- Premise: Willie is hyperactive in the classroom.
- Conclusion: If Willie takes Ritalin, his academic performance will improve.
- Warrant: In a study that compared children with the same kinds of learning problems, some of whom received Ritalin and some of whom did not, no difference in long-term academic achievement was found (Weber, Frankenberger, & Heilman, 1992).

An argument is unsound if (1) there is something wrong with its logical structure, (2) it contains false premises, or (3) it is irrelevant or circular. Can you identify counterarguments to the argument just presented? Are there "rival hypotheses"?

Exhibit 2

Evaluating Arguments: What Do You Think?

- I think her being abused as a child caused this parent to mistreat her children. That's what she learned as a child. That's all she knew.
- If Constance developed insight into her past relationships with her father, she would understand how she contributed to the problems in her own marriage and could then resolve her problems.
- If he could get money to establish a community service agency, the problems of our neighborhood would decrease because then we could fund needed programs.
- Cognitive behavioral methods will best serve this client because her negative self-statements contribute to her substance abuse.
- His authoritarian personality contributes to his problem as a community leader; he won't be able to change because that's the way he wants to be.

RECOGNIZE INFORMAL FALLACIES

Knowledge of fallacies and skill in spotting them will help you avoid dubious claims and unsound arguments. A fallacy is a mistake in thinking. Fallacies result in defective arguments (as when the premises do not provide an adequate basis for a conclusion). Fallacies that evade the facts appear to address them but do not. For instance, variants of "begging the question" include alleged certainty and circular reasoning. Vacuous guarantees may be offered, such as assuming that because a condition ought to be, it is the case, without providing support for the position. In the fallacy called "sweeping generalization," a rule or assumption that is valid in general is applied to a specific example for which it is not valid. Consider, for example, the assertion that parents abused as children abuse their own children. In fact, a large percentage of them do not. Other fallacies distort facts or positions, as in "straw-person arguments," in which an opponent's view is misrepresented, usually to make it easier to attack. Diversions such as trivial points, irrelevant objections, or emotional appeals may be used to direct attention away from the main point of an argument. Some fallacies work by creating confusion, such as feigned lack of understanding and excessive wordiness that obscures arguments.

RECOGNIZE PROPAGANDA STRATAGEMS

A stratagem is an approach used to persuade others of the truth of an assertion, to influence them to draw a certain conclusion, or to get "the better of an opponent in a dispute" (Nickerson, 1986, p. 103). Examples include misrepresenting positions, deceptive use of truth (telling only part of the truth), relying on slogans, and using putdowns. Propaganda stratagems are used to persuade, that is, to convince someone to do or believe a certain thing. People who use stratagems often attempt to persuade not by a clear argument, but indirectly, by subtle associations (e.g., enticing social workers to buy malpractice insurance by alluding to lawsuits). Such persuasive appeals do not rely on reason or logic.

The purpose of propaganda is not to inform but to persuade—to encourage belief or action with the least thought possible (Ellul, 1965). Advertisements for "therapeutic advances" often rely on propaganda methods, such as using manner of presentation as a persuasive appeal. Thinking critically about claims and arguments will help you to spot propaganda.

RECOGNIZE PSEUDOSCIENCE, FRAUD, QUACKERY

Critical thinking can help you to spot pseudoscience, fraud, and quackery more readily and thus avoid their influence. Pseudoscience refers to material that makes science-like claims but provides no evidence for them (Bunge, 1984). Quackery refers to the promotion and marketing of unproven, often worthless, and perhaps dangerous products and methods by either professionals or others (Young, 1992). Fraud refers to the intentional misrepresentation of the effect of certain actions (e.g., taking a medicine to relieve depression) to induce people to part with something of value (e.g., their money). It involves deception and misrepresentation (Miller & Hersen, 1992).

USE LANGUAGE THOUGHTFULLY

Language is so important in critical thinking that Perkins (1992) uses the phrase "language of thoughtfulness" to highlight its role. Language is important whether you speak, write, or use tools such as graphics (see Exercise 21). The degree to which a "culture of thoughtfulness" exists is reflected in the language used. For example, if terms are not clarified, confused discussions may result from the assumption of one word, one meaning. Examples of vague terms that may have quite different definitions include *abuse, aggression,* and *addiction.* Using a descriptive term as an explanatory one offers an illusion of understanding without providing any real understanding. For instance, a teacher may say that a student is aggressive. When asked to explain how she knows this, she may say he hits other children. If then asked why she thinks he hits them, she may say, "Because he is aggressive." Technical terms may be carelessly used, resulting in "bafflegarb" or "psychobabble"—words that sound informative but are of little or no use in making sound decisions. People often misuse speculation, that is, they assume that what is true can be discovered by merely thinking about it.

Recognize Affective Influences

Some fallacies could also be classified as social psychological strategies of persuasion; these work through people's affective reactions rather than through thoughtful consideration of positions related to a topic. For example, because you like to please people you like, you may be reluctant to question their use of unfounded authority.

People often try to persuade others by offering reasons that play on their emotions and appeal to accepted beliefs and values. Social psychological appeals are used by propagandists who wish to encourage action and belief with as little thought as possible (Ellul, 1965). Affective influences based on liking (e.g., the "buddy-buddy syndrome") or fear may dilute the quality of decisions made in case conferences (Dingwall, Eekelar, & Murphy, 1983; Meehl, 1973). People may be pressured into maintaining a position by being told that if they do not, they are not consistent with prior beliefs or actions—as if they could not (or should not) change their minds. Other social psychological persuasion strategies include appeals to scarcity—if you don't act now, a valuable opportunity may be lost. Many work through appeals to fear—for example, arguing against intrusion into family life to protect children because this would result in further invasions of privacy.

Learning how to recognize and counter these and other social psychological persuasion strategies is valuable when people are deciding what to believe and how to act (Cialdini, 1984). Labels such as "personality disorder" may have emotional effects that get in the way of making sound practice decisions. Consider also labels given to clients at case conferences, such as "baby batterer," which may influence judgments in ways that interfere with sound decision making (Dingwall, et al., 1983). People are influenced by their mood changes (Salovey & Turk, 1988). Positive affect is associated with creative problem solving (Isen, 1987). Stress and anxiety created by the context in which we think, such as noisy offices and work overload, may also interfere with reasoning.

Avoid Cognitive Biases

Critical thinking will help you avoid cognitive biases that may lead to unsound decisions. Examples of these biases include these tendencies: to accept initial assumptions without question, to think that causes are similar to their effects, and to underestimate the frequency of coincidences (chance occurrences). You will learn about these cognitive biases in this workbook's exercises. Attitudes and values associated with critical thinking (e.g., a commitment to reflect on the soundness of reasoning and a respect for the views of others) increase the likelihood of avoiding cognitive biases.

Increase Self-Awareness

Critical thinking and self-awareness go hand in hand. Nickerson (1986) argues that knowledge about oneself is one of the three kinds of knowledge central to critical thinking. Critical thinking requires making inferences explicit and examining them. What do I believe? Why do I believe it? Can I make a well-reasoned argument for my position? Critical think-ing encourages you to ask questions about your beliefs, values, claims, and arguments (see Exhibit 2). It encourages you to be aware of what you know and don't know and to reflect on why you act in certain ways and what the consequences may be.

RELATED SKILLS, KNOWLEDGE, AND VALUES
Skills, knowledge, values, and attitudes related to critical thinking are reviewed next.

RELATED SKILLS

Skills involved in critical thinking include detecting differences and similarities, critically evaluating arguments and claims, devising tests of claims, and conceptualizing. Identifying recurrent patterns of interaction among family members requires skills in observing these patterns. To make inferences about the causes of behavior, social workers have to synthesize the data they collect. They evaluate outcomes. These basic skills are also involved in evaluating arguments and claims and making practice decisions.

KNOWLEDGE

Three kinds of knowledge are important in critical thinking (Nickerson, 1986). One concerns critical thinking itself. Two others are domain-specific knowledge and self-knowledge.

Domain-specific knowledge

To think critically about a subject, you must know something about that subject. For instance, a study of decision making among physicians demonstrated the importance of knowledge of content (e.g., anatomy, bio-chemistry). The "possession of relevant bodies of information and a sufficiently broad experience with related problems to permit the deter-mination of which information is pertinent, which clinical findings are significant, and how these findings are to be integrated into appropriate hypotheses and conclusions" (Elstein, Shulman, Sprafka, Allal, Gordon, Jason, Kagan, Loupe, & Jordan, 1978) were foundation components related to competence in clinical problem solving. Knowledge is required to evaluate the plausibility of premises related to an argument. Consider the following example:

- Depression always has a psychological cause.
- Mr. Draper is depressed.
- Therefore, the cause of Mr. Draper's depression is psychological.

Though the logic of this argument is sound, the conclusion may be false. Experience with depressed persons could help you identify cases of depression caused by a physiological problem. The more that is known in an area (the greater the knowledge that can decrease uncertainty about what decision is best), the more important it is to be familiar with this knowledge. Thus, just as domain-specific knowledge is necessary but insufficient for thinking effectively about many questions, clear-thinking skills cannot replace knowledge of content.

Self-knowledge

Critical thinking requires thinking about your thinking process. The term *meta-cognitive* refers to knowledge about your reasoning process (awareness and influence over your reasoning process). To think about your thinking, you might ask questions such as How am I doing? Is this correct? How do I know this is true? Do I really understand this point? These questions highlight the self-correcting role of critical thinking. Increasingly meta-cognitive levels of thought include the following:

- *Tacit use:* thinking without thinking about it
- *Aware use:* thinking and being conscious that one is thinking and when
- *Strategic use:* thinking is organized with particular conscious strategies that enhance its effectiveness
- *Reflective use:* "reflecting on our thinking before and after—or even in the middle of—the process, pondering how to proceed and how to improve" (Schwartz & Perkins, 1990, p. 52)

Self-knowledge includes familiarity with the strengths and limitations of reasoning processes in general as well as a knowledge of your personal strengths and limitations that influence how you approach problem solving and decision making. Resources include self-criticism (e.g., asking What are my biases?) Is there another way this problem could be structured? as well as tools (e.g., drawing diagrams of an argument). Three of the basic building blocks of reasoning suggested by Paul in Exhibit 1—ideas and concepts drawn on, whatever is taken for granted, and the point of view in which one's thinking is embedded—concern background knowledge important to consider because it influences how we approach problems. Self-criticism allows us to discover and correct faulty assumptions. Without this, unrecognized preconceptions can interfere with making sound judgments.

RELATED VALUES, ATTITUDES, AND DISPOSITIONS

Critical thinking involves more than the mere possession of related knowledge and skills. It requires using them in everyday situations and acting on the results (Paul, 1993). Predispositions and attitudes related to critical thinking include fairmindedness and openmindedness, a respect for the opinion of others, a desire to be well informed, a tendency to think before acting, and curiosity (Baron, 1985; Ennis, 1987; Nickerson, 1988–1989). These attitudes are related to underlying values regarding human rights and the dignity and intrinsic worth of all human beings (Baron, 1985; Brookfield, 1987; Nickerson, 1986). Related values, attitudes, and dispositions are listed in Exhibits 3 and 4. Many cognitive styles, attitudes, and strategies associated with creativity are also involved in critical thinking, including a readiness to explore and to change, and attention to problem finding as well as immersion in a task (Greeno, 1989; Nickerson, et al., 1985; Weisberg, 1986).

Exhibit 3

*Values and Attitudes
Related to Critical Thinking*

- Believe in and respect human rights and the dignity and intrinsic worth of all human beings.
- Respect the truth above self-interest.
- Value learning and critical discussion.
- Respect opinions that differ from your own. Value tolerance and open-mindedness in which you seriously consider other points of view; reason from premises with which you disagree without letting the disagreement interfere with reasoning; withhold judgment when the evidence and reasons are insufficient.
- Value being well informed.
- Seek reasons for beliefs and claims.
- Rely on sound evidence.
- Consider the total situation.
- Remain relevant to the main point.
- Seek alternatives.
- Take a position (and change it) when the evidence and reasons are sufficient to do so.
- Seek clarity.
- Deal in an orderly manner with the parts of a complex whole.
- Be sensitive to the feelings, level of knowledge, and degree of sophistication of others.
- Think independently.
- Persevere in seeking clarity and evaluating arguments.

Source: Paul (1993). See also Ennis (1987), Popper (1972).

Exhibit 4

Valuable Intellectual Traits

- *Intellectual humility* Recognizing the limits of one's knowledge, including a sensitivity to circumstances in which one's native egocentrism is likely to function self-deceptively; sensitivity to bias, prejudice and limitations of one's viewpoint. Intellectual humility depends on recognizing that one should not claim more than one actually knows. It does not imply spine-lessness or submissiveness. It implies the lack of intellectual pretentious-ness, boastfulness, or conceit, combined with insight into the logical foundations, or lack of such foundations, or one's beliefs.
- *Intellectual courage* Facing and fairly addressing ideas, beliefs or view-points toward which we have strong negative emotions and to which we have not given a serious hearing. This courage is connected with the recognition that ideas considered dangerous or absurd may be reasonable and that our conclusions and beliefs are sometimes false or misleading. To determine for ourselves which is which, we must not passively and uncritically "accept" what we have "learned." Intellectual courage comes into play here, because inevitably we will come to see some truth in some ideas strongly held in our social group. We need courage to be true to our own thinking in such circumstances. The penalties for non-conformity can be severe.
- *Intellectual empathy* Being aware of the need to imaginatively put oneself in the place of others in order to genuinely understand them,

Exhibit 4
(continued)

which requires the consciousness of our egocentric tendency to identify truth with our immediate perceptions of long-standing thought or belief. This trait correlates with the ability to reconstruct accurately the viewpoints and reasoning of others and to reason from premises, assumptions, and ideas other than our own. This trait also correlates with the willingness to remember occasions when we were wrong in the past despite an intense conviction that we were right, and with the ability to imagine our being similarly deceived in a case-at-hand.

- *Intellectual integrity* Recognition of the need to be consistent in the intellectual standards one applies; to hold one's self to the same rigorous standards of evidence and proof to which one holds one's antagonists; to practice what one advocates for others; and to honestly admit discrepancies and inconsistencies in one's own thought and action.
- *Intellectual perseverance* Using intellectual insights and truths in spite of difficulties, obstacles, and frustrations; firm adherence to rational principles despite the irrational opposition of others; a sense of the need to struggle with confusion and unsettled questions over an extended period of time to achieve deeper understanding or insight.
- *Confidence in reason* Confidence that, in the long run, one's own higher interests and those of humankind at large will be best served by giving the freest play to reason, by encouraging people to develop their rational faculties; faith that, with proper encouragement and cultivation, people can learn to think for themselves, to form rational viewpoints, draw reasonable conclusions, think coherently and logically, persuade each other by reason and become reasonable persons, despite the deep-seated obstacles to doing so.
- *Fairmindedness* Treating all viewpoints alike, without reference to one's own feelings or vested interests, or the feelings or vested interests of one's friends, community or nation; implies adherence to intellectual standards without reference to one's own advantage or the advantage of one's group.

Source: Richard Paul (1994). Paper distributed at the 14th International Conference on Critical Thinking, Sonoma, CA. See Paul, 1993.

Critical thinkers question what others take for granted. They may ask people to support assumptions that others believe to be self-evident, but which are far from being self-evident. They ask, "What's the evidence for ————?" Critical thinking encourages open dialogue and the consideration of opposing views. It involves taking responsibility for claims made and arguments presented. It requires flexibility and a readiness to admit, even welcome, the discovery of mistakes in your thinking. Critical thinking is independent thinking—thinking for yourself. Critical thinkers question values and positions that may be common in a society, in a group, or in their own family.

HELPFUL DISTINCTIONS IN THINKING CRITICALLY ABOUT PRACTICE BELIEFS AND DECISIONS

The distinctions described in this section will help you to arrive at well-reasoned practice beliefs and actions.

WIDELY ACCEPTED/TRUE

What is *widely accepted* may not be *true*. Consider the following exchange:

- Ms. Simmons (social worker): I've referred this client to the adolescent stress service because this agency is widely used.
- Ms. Harris (supervisor): Do you know anything about how effective this agency is in helping adolescents like your client?
- Ms. Simmons: They receive more referrals than any other agency for these kinds of problems. They are successful in helping clients. We're lucky if they accept my client.

Many people believe in the influence of astrological signs (their causal role is widely accepted). However, to date, there is no evidence that they have a causal role in influencing behavior (Dean, 1986–1987), that is, risky predictions based on related beliefs have not survived critical tests. Can you think of some other beliefs that are widely accepted but not true?

A FEELING THAT SOMETHING IS TRUE VERSUS WHETHER IT IS TRUE

Another helpful distinction is between a "feeling" that something is true and whether it is true. Not making this distinction helps to account for the widespread belief in many questionable causes of behavior such as astrological influences, crystals, spirit guides, and so on (see for example Dean, 1987). People use their "feeling" that something is true as a criterion to accept or reject possible causes. However, a "feeling" that something is true may not (and often does not) correspond to what *is* true.

REASONING/RATIONALIZING

Reasoning involves reviewing the evidence both against and in favor of a position. *Rationalizing* is a selective search for evidence in support of a belief or action. This selective search may occur either automatically (without our awareness) or deliberately. When people rationalize, they focus on building a case rather than weighing evidence for and against an argument. This is not to say that there is no interest in persuading others about the soundness of our arguments. The difference lies in the means used.

JUSTIFIABLE/FALSIFIABLE

Many people accept a justificationist approach to knowledge development. They focus on gathering support for justifying claims, theories, and arguments. Let's say that you see 3,000 swans, and they are all white. Does this mean that *all* swans are white? Can you generalize from the particular (seeing 3,000 swans, all of which are white) to the general ("All swans are white.")? Karl Popper (and others) argue that people cannot discover what is true by induction (generalizing from the particular to the general) because they may later discover exceptions (some swans that are not white). In fact, black swans *are* found in some parts of the world. Popper argues that falsification (attempts to falsify, to discover the errors in our beliefs) via critical tests of claims is the only sound way to develop knowledge (see for example Popper, 1992; 1994). People subject their beliefs to critical tests to discover errors, and learn from these errors to make more informed guesses in the future. He suggests that people do not know more today than they did thousands of years ago because solving some problems creates new ones. For example, medical advances have created new problems such as population growth, which strains resources.

TRUTH AND CREDIBILITY

Karl Popper defines truthful statements as those that correspond with the facts. Credible statements are those that are possible to believe. Dennis Phillips (1992) points out that just about anything may be credible. This does not mean that it is true. Thus the distinction between truth and credibility is an important one. Simply because it is possible to believe something does not mean that it is true. Although the purpose of science is to seek true answers to problems (statements that correspond to the facts), this does not mean that there is certain knowledge. Rather, people may say that certain beliefs (theories) have (so far) survived critical tests or have not yet been exposed to them. An error "consists essentially of our regarding as true a theory that is not true" (Popper, 1992, p. 4). People can avoid error or discover it by doing all they can to discover and eliminate falsehoods (p. 4).

PERSONAL KNOWLEDGE
AND OBJECTIVE KNOWLEDGE

Personal knowledge refers to what you as an individual "know." Objective knowledge refers to points of view that have survived critical tests or evaluation. It is public. It is criticizable by others.

WHAT TO THINK AND HOW TO THINK

Critics of the educational system argue that students are too often told *what* to think and do not learn *how* to think. Thinking critically about your beliefs requires you to examine how you think. This is quite different from memorizing a list of alleged facts. Examining the accuracy of these facts requires thinking critically about them.

PROPAGANDA BIAS/
INFORMED POINT OF VIEW

Bias refers to an emotional leaning to one side. Biased people who try to persuade others may or may not be aware that they are doing so. They may use faulty reasoning to gain an uncritical, emotional acceptance of a position. Or they may use propaganda strategies designed to encourage action with the least thought possible (Ellul, 1965). Here are some common propaganda tactics:

- Appeal to emotions
- Urge immediate action "while the chance still lasts" to discourage taking time to reason about the evidence
- Present only one side of the argument
- Include a mixture of strong and weak evidence only so long as it supports a favored conclusion or course of action
- Deflect any criticism by attacking the motives of the critic (e.g., anyone who doubts the effectiveness of our treatment for battered women must be trying to undermine our efforts to help women)
- Resort to any argument, no matter how illogical, to persuade others

People with an informed point of view are also aware of their interests, but they describe their sources, state their views clearly, and avoid using propaganda devices. Their statements and questions encourage rather than discourage critical review. They will clarify their statements when asked to do so.

REASONING/TRUTH

Reasoning does not necessarily yield the *truth*. "People who are considered by many of their peers to be reasonable people often do take, and are able to defend quite convincingly, diametrically opposing positions on controversial matters" (Nickerson, 1986, p. 12). However, effective reasoners are more likely to critically examine their views than ineffective reasoners. Also, the accuracy of a conclusion does not necessarily indicate that the reasoning used to reach it was sound. For example, errors in the opposite direction may have cancelled each other out. Lack of evidence for a claim does not mean that it is incorrect. Similarly, surviving critical tests does not mean that a claim is true. Further tests may show that it is false (Popper, 1994).

REASONING/PERSUASION

Both reasoning and persuasive appeals are used to encourage people to act or think in a certain way. *Reasoning* involves a *critical evaluation of claims*. The major intent of persuasion is not to inform or to arrive at the soundest decision, but to encourage thought or action. Persuasive appeals can be viewed as a subset of those strategies used to encourage certain beliefs or actions. They include propagandistic methods such as appeals to fear or scarcity (see for example Cialdini, 1984).

CONSISTENCY, CORROBORATION, AND PROOF

Assigning proper weight to different kinds of evidence is a key part of what it means to be reasonable. Distinguishing between consistency, corroboration, and proof will help you do this. People often use *consistency*, or agreement among different sources of data, to support their beliefs. For example, they may say that Mrs. X is depressed currently because she has a prior history of depression. However, saying that A (a history of "depression") is consistent with B (alleged current "depression") is to say only that it is possible to believe B given A. Two or more assertions thus may be consistent with each other but yield little or no insight into the soundness of an argument.

Proof implies certainty about a claim, as in the statement, "The effectiveness of management services to the frail elderly has been proven in this study." Since future tests may show an assumption to be incorrect, even one that is strongly *corroborated,* no assertion can ever be proven (Popper, 1972). If nothing can ever be proven, the least that can be done is to construct theories that are falsifiable: theories that generate specific hypotheses that can be tested.

Some claims are not falsifiable; that is, there is no way to find out if they are correct. Psychoanalytic theory is often criticized on the grounds that it is not falsifiable—that contradictory hypotheses can be drawn from the theory. As Popper (1959) points out, irrefutability is not a virtue of a theory, but a vice.

BELIEFS, OPINIONS, AND FACTS

A *belief* can be defined as "confidence that a particular thing is true as evidenced by a willingness to act as though it were" (Nickerson, 1986, p. 2). Beliefs are statements that can be shown to be false. Beliefs as guesses about what may be true or false are quite different than beliefs as convictions that are not open to criticism. *Facts* can be defined as beliefs that have been critically evaluated and/or tested. In a scientific approach it is assumed that the accuracy of an assertion is related to the uniqueness and supportive value of predictions that have been tested. Facts are capable of falsification (shown that they are not true); beliefs may not be. *Opinions* are statements of preferences and values. It does not make sense to consider opinions as true or false, because people differ in their preferences, as in the statement, "I prefer insight-oriented treatment." This differs from the statement, "Play therapy can help children overcome anxiety," which reflects a belief because evidence can be gathered to find out if it is accurate. Other examples of opinions and beliefs are shown below. The first one is an opinion. The last two are beliefs.

- I like to collect payment for each session at the end of the session.
- Insight therapy is more effective than cognitive-behavioral treatment of depression.
- My pet Rottweiler helps people with their problems (quote from a psychologist on a morning talk show, 4/6/88).

SCIENTIFIC REASONING

Both critical thinking and scientific reasoning provide a way of thinking about and testing assumptions that is of special value to those in helping roles, such as social workers. Both share a reliance on shared standards that encourage you to challenge assumptions, consider opposing points of view, be precise, and check for errors. Science is often misrepresented. Common misconceptions include the following:

- There is a search for final answers.
- Intuitive thinking has no role.
- It is assumed that science knows or will soon know all the answers.
- Objectivity is assumed.
- Chance occurrences are not assumed.
- Scientific knowledge is equivalent to scientific thinking.
- Linear thinking is required.
- Passion and caring have no role.

Some present science as a set of facts or as referring only to controlled experimental studies.

Science is a problem-solving process that emphasizes the critical testing of claims. It offers procedures for trying to answer certain kinds of questions. Science provides a way of thinking about and investigating the accuracy of assumptions about the world. It is a *process*. The essence of science is guessing and testing, identifying problems and trying to solve them in a way that offers accurate information about whether a conjecture (a guess or theory) is correct (Asimov, 1989). The terms *science* and *scientific* are sometimes used to refer to any systematic effort to acquire information about a subject. They include case, correlational, and naturalistic studies. Nonexperimental approaches to understanding events and behaviors involve observation—for example, relationships can be found between a behavior and its consequences.

HALLMARKS OF SCIENTIFIC REASONING

Scientists search for patterns and regularities

Scientists assume that there is consistency in the universe. They search for patterns and regularities. This does not mean that unexplained phenomena or chance variations do not occur. Uncertainty is assumed. Approximations to the truth are valued (Popper, 1994).

Scientists make their own observations

Consider the old question of how many teeth are in a horse's mouth. One could either speculate about this or open the horse's mouth and look inside. Let's say an agency for the homeless claims that it succeeds in finding homes for applicants within ten days. You could accept this claim on face value or else actually see for yourself if this assertion is true. Observation is often structured to increase the likelihood that results will yield valuable information, as described in the next section.

Scientists design critical tests of theories

The constant interplay between theories and their testing is central to science. For example, an assumption that verbal instructions can help decrease smoking could be tested by randomly assigning smokers to an experimental group (receiving such instructions) and a control group (not receiving instructions) and observing their behavior to see what happens. Let's say that you think you will learn some specific skills in a class you are taking. You might apply scientific thinking to your question.

You could assess your skills before the class and after the class and see if your skills have increased. Testing your belief will offer more information than simply thinking about it. What if you find that your skills have increased? Does this show that the class was responsible for your new skills? It does not, because there are other possible causes, or *rival hypotheses*. For example, maybe you learned these skills in some other context. Scientists are often wrong and find out they are wrong by testing their predictions.

Popper (1959) argues that falsifiability is an important characteristic of any assertion or theory. Claims can only be falsified if specific predictions are made. In Popper's view, scientific statements are those statements that are testable, in terms of being refutable. Thus, explanations that are untestable are problematic. "A scientific theory...must specify not only what is and what can happen, but...what *cannot* be, what cannot happen, according to its logic as well" (Monte, 1975, p. 93). Can you make accurate predictions based on a belief? Falsifiability is emphasized as more critical than confirmation because the latter is easier to obtain. Scientists assume that nothing is ever "proven" (Miller, 1994; Popper, 1972).

Scientists revere parsimony

Scientists prefer accounts that avoid unnecessary concepts. An explanation is parsimonious only if the fewest components are required to explain the most related phenomena. Unnecessarily complex explanations may take us far afield from the observed data and get in the way of detecting relationships between behaviors of interest and environmental events that could be altered in order to remove complaints. Consider the following accounts of a mother's reaction:

1. Mrs. Lancer punishes her child because of unresolved superego issues related to early childhood trauma. This creates a negative disposition toward her oldest child.
2. Mrs. Lancer hits her child because this removes his annoying behaviors temporarily (he stops yelling) and because she does not possess positive parenting skills (e.g., identifying and reinforcing behaviors she wants to see more of).

In the second account, attention is drawn to environmental factors related to Mrs. Lancer's actions and to specific behaviors that could be altered. It is not clear that reliance on concepts such as "unresolved superego issues" and "negative disposition" yield specific guidelines for altering complaints; therefore, the first account is not parsimonious.

Scientists demonstrate a skeptical attitude

An open yet skeptical attitude is a key characteristic of scientific thinking. Skeptics are more interested in arriving at accurate answers (those that are most likely to help clients attain desired outcomes) than in not ruffling the feathers of supervisors or administrators. They value critical discussion because it can reveal flaws in their own thinking about a problem, which should enable better guesses about what is true, and these in turn can be tested. Knowledge is viewed as tentative. Scientists question what others view as fact or "common sense." Skepticism does not imply cynicism (being negative about everything). Scientists willingly change their beliefs if additional evidence demands it. Openness to criticism is a key hallmark of scientific thinking. Karl Popper considers it the mark of rationality.

Scientists strive for objectivity

Karl Popper (1994) argues that "the so-called objectivity of science lies in the objectivity of the critical method; that is, above all, in the fact that no theory is exempt from criticism, and further, in the fact that the logical instrument of criticism—the logical contradiction—is objective" (p. 67). Objectivity implies that the results of science are independent of any one scientist so that different people exploring the same problem will reach the same conclusions. It is assumed that perception is theory-laden (influenced by people's expectations). This assumption has been well accepted in science for some time (see for example Phillips, 1987, 1992). People often confuse values external to science (e.g., what should be) with values internal to science (e.g., critical testing) (Phillips, 1987).

Scientists address solvable problems

Science deals with specific problems that are solvable—they can potentially be answered given the available methods of empirical inquiry. Examples include the following: Is intensive in-home care for parents of abused children more effective than the usual social work services? And is use of medication to decrease depression in elderly people more (or less) effective than cognitive-behavioral methods? Examples of unsolvable questions include Should punishment ever be used in raising children? and Are people inherently good or evil? Saying that science deals with problems that are solvable does not mean that other kinds of questions are unimportant or that a problem will remain unsolvable. New methods may be developed that allow pursuit of questions previously unapproachable in a systematic way.

Scientists share knowledge freely

Scientific knowledge is public—for all to use. Science is *collective*. That is, scientists communicate with one another, and the results of later scientific efforts are informed by earlier ones.

SCIENCE AND PSEUDOSCIENCE

Pseudoscience refers to science-like claims that have no evidence provided for them. A critical attitude, which Popper (1963) defines as a willingness and commitment to open up favored views to severe scrutiny, is basic to science. This attitude distinguishes science from pseudoscience, which is characterized by a casual approach to evidence: weak evidence is accepted as readily as strong. Here are other hallmarks of pseudoscience (Bunge, 1984; Gray, 1991):

- discourages the critical examination of claims/arguments
- uses the trappings of science without the substance
- relies on anecdotal evidence
- is not self-correcting

- is unskeptical
- equates an open mind with an uncritical one
- ignores or explains away falsifying data
- relies on vague language
- produces beliefs and faith but not knowledge
- is often not testable
- does not require repeatability

Irrefutable hypotheses may be accompanied by a reluctance to revise beliefs, even when confronted with relevant criticism. Excessive claims of contributions to knowledge are often made, as well as multiple references to a source until that source achieves the status of a law.

Pseudoscience is a billion-dollar industry. Products include self-help books, "subliminal" tapes, and call-in psychic advice from "authentic psychics" (Druckman & Bjork, 1991; Leahey & Leahey, 1983). Pseudo-science can be found in all fields, including multiculturalism (see for example Oritz De Montellano, 1992). Proselytizers of many sorts base their claims on bogus references to science. Advertisers use the trappings of science (without the substance) to encourage consumers to buy products (see for example Young, 1992).

The term *science* has been applied to many activities that really have nothing to do with science. Examples include "scientific charity" and "scientific philanthropy." Basaglia argues that the ideology and "trappings" of science are used to pull the wool over people's eyes by suggesting a critical testing of claims that has not been carried out (Scheper-Hughes & Lovell, 1987). Classification of clients into psychiatric categories lends an aura of science to this practice, whether or not there is any evidence that this is helpful to clients (Kirk & Kutchins, 1992).

Exhibit 5 (pp. 24–25) defines some terms related to science and pseudo-science. Quack reasoning reflects pseudoscience. A quack

1. Promises quick, dramatic, miraculous cures
2. Speaks imprecisely and vaguely to describe a client's problem and intended outcome
3. Employs anecdotes and testimonials to support claims
4. Is bound to a particular dogma, theory, or set of beliefs, and does not alter them based on new evidence
5. Objects to testing claims
6. Forwards methods and theories that are not consistent with natural laws as we now understand them
7. Joins cults that follow the techniques of a charismatic individual and in which members consider themselves among the faithful
8. Claims his or her methods cannot be tested by usually accepted methods of investigation (e.g., clinical trials)
9. Mixes bona fide and bogus evidence so the evidence supports a favored conclusion (see for example Herbert, 1983; Jarvis, 1990; McCain & Segal, 1988)

Millions of dollars are spent by consumers on worthless products. Natale (1988) estimated that in 1987 Americans spent $50 million on subliminal tapes. There is no evidence that these offer what they promise

(Druckman & Bjork, 1991). Fraud is so extensive in some areas that special organizations have been formed and newsletters written to help consumers evaluate claims (for example, *Health Letter,* published by Public Citizen Health Research Group). For every claim supported by critical testing, there are scores of bogus claims in advertisements, newscasts, films, TV, newspapers, and professional sources, whose lures are difficult to resist.

REVIEWING THE COSTS AND BENEFITS OF CRITICAL THINKING

The benefits of critical thinking include discovering better alternatives, enhancing the quality of decision-making skills, and reaching moral decisions in which the interests of all involved parties are considered. You will be more likely to discard irrelevant, misleading, and incomplete accounts that may result in harm to clients. Here is a summary of the benefits:

You will be more likely to

1. Ask questions with a high payoff
2. Select valid assessment methods
3. Describe problems and related factors accurately
4. Make accurate assumptions about causes related to problems
5. Choose relevant outcomes to focus on
6. Select intervention methods that are likely to be successful
7. Make accurate predictions
8. Make sound decisions at case conferences
9. Choose sound policies
10. Distinguish between possible and impossible jobs
11. Continue to learn and enhance learning skills

Because you will

1. Recognize weak appeals
2. Recognize propaganda
3. Identify pseudoscience and quackery
4. Use tests effectively
5. Use language effectively
6. Avoid cognitive biases
7. Identify personal obstacles to critical thinking
8. Identify environmental obstacles to a culture of thoughtfulness

Some of the costs of thinking carefully include "ruffling others' feathers," foregoing the comfortable feeling of "certainty," and the time and effort required to consider opposing views (Gambrill, 1990). Many of the costs of not thinking critically about practice-related claims and arguments are hidden. By not looking carefully you are not as likely to discover inaccurate beliefs or ignored or suppressed knowledge such as harms done in the guise of helping. Curiosity is likely to languish if vague, oversimplified accounts are accepted that obscure the complexity of issues, giving an illusion of understanding and offering no guidelines for helping clients. Furthermore, unwanted sources of control may continue to be influential if they remain hidden, and clients are less likely to receive effective services.

Thus, being a critical thinker will require overcoming many barriers. Personal barriers include lack of education in related knowledge, skills, and attitudes, as well as misunderstanding scientific reasoning. Critical thinkers often encounter a hostile environment that perceives critical thinking as a threat to current beliefs. Others may turn a seemingly deaf ear to embarrassing questions, such as What evidence is there for your belief? or Could there be another explanation? It is not in the interests of many groups (e.g., advertisers, politicians, professional organizations) to reveal the lack of evidence for claims made and policies recommended. Some people believe that good intentions are enough. This belief may be combined with extreme relativism, or the belief that all methods are equally good because there is no way of discovering what works best, when in fact this may be untrue.

Decisions about whether or not to think carefully about a topic or problem will be influenced by your history. Has thinking paid off in the past? If you believe that little can be done about a problem, you probably won't spend much time thinking about how to resolve it. If you believe that you are helpless, you will act helpless. The stark realities that confront social workers and the assumption that nothing can change may result in workers not thinking about decisions that influence the quality of service. However, this starkness itself is a compelling reason to take advantage of critical-thinking skills.

SUMMARY

Critical thinking will help you to make sound practice decisions. The purpose of social work practice is to help clients achieve outcomes they value, whether clients be individuals, families, organizations, or communities. Keeping an eye on this basic purpose is key to critical thinking. Critical thinking, knowledge, skills, and values can help you evaluate the credibility of claims and arguments, use language effectively, and avoid cognitive biases that interfere with sound decision making. As a critical thinker, you will spot pseudoscience and quackery more readily. This in turn should help you to offer more effective services to your clients. Critical thinking will help you choose wisely among options—to select those that, compared with others, are most likely to help clients attain specific outcomes.

Critical thinking involves a careful appraisal of claims, a fair-minded consideration of alternative views, and a willingness to change your mind in light of evidence that refutes a cherished position. Assumptions are questioned in both critical thinking and scientific reasoning. Differences are viewed as opportunities to learn. Both value testing as well as guessing. Critical thinking and scientific reasoning are especially important in professions such as social work, where clients confront real-life problems. Related knowledge, skills, and attitudes can help you to avoid misleading directions from relying on questionable criteria such as appeals to unfounded authority, popularity, or manner of presentation.

Exhibit 5

Glossary

- *Critical discussion* "Essentially a comparison of the merits and demerits of two or more theories. . . . The merits discussed are mainly the *explanatory power* of the theories . . . the way in which they are able to solve our problems and explain things, the way in which the theories cohere with certain other heavily valued theories, their power to shed new light on old problems and to suggest new problems. The chief demerit is inconsistency, including inconsistency with the results of experiments that a competing theory can explain" (Popper, 1994, pp. 160–161).
- *Cynicism* A negative view of the world and what can be learned about it.
- *Eclecticism* The view that people should adopt whatever theories or methodologies are useful in inquiry, no matter their source, and without undue worry about their consistency.
- *Empiricism* "The position that all knowledge (usually, but not always, excluding that which is logico-mathematical) is in some way 'based upon' experience. Adherents of empiricism differ markedly over what the 'based upon' amounts to—'starts from' and 'warranted in terms of' are, roughly, at the two ends of the spectrum of opinion" (Phillips, 1987, p. 203).
- *Hermeneutics* "The discipline of interpretation of textual or literary material, or of meaningful human actions" (Phillips, 1987, p. 203).
- *Knowledge* Problematic and tentative guesses about what may be true (Popper, 1992, 1994).
- *Logical positivism* The main tenet is the verifiability principle of meaning: "Something is meaningful only if it is verifiable empirically (i.e., directly, or indirectly, via sense experiences) or if it is a truth of logic or mathematics" (Phillips, 1987, p. 204). The reality of purely theoretical entities is denied.
- *Nonjustificationist epistemology* The view that knowledge is not certain. It is assumed that although some knowledge claims may be warranted, there is no warrant so firm that it is not open to question (see Karl Popper's writings).
- *Paradigm* A theoretical framework that influences "the problems that are regarded as crucial, the ways these problems are conceptualized, the appropriate methods of inquiry, the relevant standards of judgment, etc." (Phillips, 1987, p. 205).
- *Phenomenology* "The study, in depth, of how things appear in human experience" (Phillips, 1987, p. 205).
- *Postpositivism* The approach to science that replaced logical positivism decades ago (see for example Phillips, 1987, 1992).
- *Pseudoscience* Material that makes sciencelike claims but provides no evidence for these claims.
- *Quackery* Commercialization of unproven, often worthless and sometimes dangerous products and procedures either by professionals or others (Jarvis, 1990; Young, 1992).
- *Relativism* The belief that a proposition can be true for individuals in one framework of belief but false for individuals in a different framework. Relativists "insist that judgments of truth are always relative to a particular framework or point of view" (Phillips, 1987, p. 206).
- *Science* A process designed to develop knowledge through critical discussion and testing of theories.
- *Scientific objectivity* This "consists solely in the critical approach" (Popper, 1994, p. 93). It is based on mutual rational criticism in which high standards of clarity and rational criticism are valued (Popper, 1994, p. 70)(see also *Critical discussion*, above).

Exhibit 5
(continued)

- *Scientism* This term is used "to indicate slavish adherence to the methods of science even in a context where they are inappropriate" and "to indicate a false or mistaken claim to be scientific" (Phillips, 1987, p. 206).
- *Skepticism* The belief that all claims should be carefully examined for invalid arguments and errors of fact.
- *Theory* Myths, expectations, guesses, conjectures about what may be true. A theory always remains hypothetical or conjectural. "It always remains guesswork. And there is no theory that is not beset with problems" (Popper, 1994, p. 157).
- *Theory-ladenness (of perception)* "The thesis that the process of perception is theory-laden in that the observer's background knowledge (including theories, factual information, hypotheses, and so forth) acts as a 'lens' helping to 'shape' the nature of what is observed" (Phillips, 1987, p. 206).
- *Truth* "An assertion is true if it corresponds to, or agrees with, the facts" (Popper, 1994, p. 174). People can never be sure that their guesses are true. "Though we can never justify the claim to have reached truth, we can often give some very good reasons, or justifications, why one theory should be judged as nearer to it than another" (Popper, 1994, p. 161).

Exercise 1
MAKING DECISIONS ABOUT INTERVENTION

PURPOSE

Professionals have to make decisions about how to address certain problems. This exercise provides an opportunity for you to review the criteria you use to make decisions.

BACKGROUND

People in the helping professions often become so involved in the process of helping that they forget to step back and examine the basis for their decisions. This exercise encourages you to examine the criteria you use to make decisions.

INSTRUCTIONS

1. Answer the questions on pages 29–30.
2. Review your answers using the guidelines provided. To get the most out of the exercise, complete the questionnaire before you read the discussion questions.

Exhibit 1.1   **MAKING DECISIONS ABOUT INTERVENTION**

Your Name _____   Date _____

Course _____

Instructor's Name _____

SITUATION 1   *Think back to a particular client (individual, family, group, agency, or community) with whom you have worked. Place a checkmark next to each criterion <u>you used to make your practice decisions</u>. If you have not yet worked with a client to make a practice decision, think of the criteria you would probably rely on.*

CRITERIA

____ 1. Your intuition (gut feeling) about what will be effective
____ 2. What you have heard from other professionals in informal exchanges
____ 3. Your experience with a few cases
____ 4. Your demonstrated track record of success based on data you have gathered systematically and regularly
____ 5. What fits your personal style
____ 6. What was usually offered at your agency
____ 7. Self-reports of other clients about what was helpful
____ 8. Results of controlled experimental studies (data that show that a method is helpful)*
____ 9. What you are most familiar with
____ 10. What you know by critically reading professional literature

---

*Controlled experimental studies involve the random assignment of people to a group receiving a treatment method (e.g., cognitive-behavioral intervention) and one not receiving the treatment.

SITUATION 2   *Imagine that you have a potentially serious medical problem, and you seek help from a physician to examine treatment options. Place a checkmark next to each criterion <u>you would like your physician to rely on</u> when he or she makes recommendations about your treatment.*

CRITERIA

____ 1. The physician's intuition (gut feeling) that a method will work

____ 2. What he or she has heard from other physicians in informal exchanges

____ 3. The physician's experience with a few cases

____ 4. The physician's demonstrated track record of success based on data he or she has gathered systematically and regularly

____ 5. What fits his or her personal style

____ 6. What is usually offered at the clinic

____ 7. Self-reports of patients about what was helpful

____ 8. Results of controlled experimental studies (data that show that a method is helpful)

____ 9. What the physician is most familiar with

____ 10. What the physician has learned by critically reading professional literature

SITUATION 3   *Think back to a particular client (individual, family, group, agency, or community) with whom you have worked. Place a checkmark next to each criterion <u>you would like to use ideally</u> to make practice decisions. If you have not yet worked with a client to make a practice decision, think of the criteria you would ideally like to rely on.*

CRITERIA

____ 1. Your intuition (gut feeling) about what will be effective

____ 2. What you have heard from other professionals in informal exchanges

____ 3. Your experience with a few cases

____ 4. Your demonstrated track record of success based on data you have gathered systematically and regularly

____ 5. What fits your personal style

____ 6. What was usually offered at your agency

____ 7. Self-reports of other clients about what was helpful

____ 8. Results of controlled experimental studies (data that show that a method is helpful

____ 9. What you are most familiar with

____ 10. What you know by critically reading professional literature

Your instructor will provide scoring instructions.

Situation 1 (Your Actual Criteria): _____

Situation 2 (Physician's Criteria): _____

Situation 3 (Your Ideal Criteria): _____

DISCUSSION   If you scored two to ten points, you are basing your decisions on criteria likely to result in a well-reasoned judgment (results from controlled experimental studies, systematically collected data, and critical reading). If you scored below two in any of the situations, you are willing to base decisions on criteria that may result in selecting ineffective methods.

When making decisions, professionals often use different criteria in different situations. For instance, they may think more carefully in situations in which the potential consequences of their choices matter more to them personally (e.g., a health matter). Research on critical thinking shows that lack of generalization is a key problem; that is, people may use critical thinking skills in some situations but not in others (Norris, 1992).

FOLLOW-UP QUESTIONS

Do your choices differ in these situations? If so, how? Why do you think they differ? If you scored below two on Situation 1 and two or more on Situation 2, you may not believe that what's good for the goose is good for the gander. Your approach may be "science for you and art for them." If you scored below 2 in Situations 2 and 3, you may be prone to disregard sound evidence generally.

_____

_____

_____

_____

Exercise 2
REVIEWING YOUR BELIEFS ABOUT KNOWLEDGE

PURPOSE

This exercise provides an opportunity to review your beliefs about knowledge (what it is and how it can be obtained).

BACKGROUND

All professionals have to make decisions. These decisions reflect their underlying beliefs about what can be known and how it can be known. These beliefs influence how they evaluate claims concerning how best to help clients. Many exercises in this workbook concern criteria for evaluating claims (see for example Exercises 3, 4–9, 11, 12, 16, 17, and 19). Beliefs about knowledge that can get in the way of critically evaluating claims are described in this exercise. It also suggests replies to objections to the view that people can (and do) know something about the world.

INSTRUCTIONS

1. Answer the questions in on pages 35–38 by circling the response that most accurately reflects your view (A = Agree; D = Disagree; N = No opinion). Write a brief explanation below each statement or on a separate sheet of paper to explain why you circled the response you did.
2. Compare your replies with ones that will be provided by your instructor.

Exhibit 2.1   **REVIEWING YOUR BELIEFS ABOUT KNOWLEDGE**

Your Name   Date
_____

Course
_____

Instructor's Name
_____

A = Agree   **D** = Disagree   **N** = No Opinion

_____

1. Since we can't know anything for sure,   **A   D   N**
   we really don't know anything.

2. Since our beliefs influence what we see,   **A   D   N**
   we can't gather accurate knowledge about
   our world.

3. There are things we just can't know.   **A   D   N**

_____

Note: Items 3–9 are based on W. Gray (1991), *Thinking critically about new age ideas*. Belmont,
Calif.: Wadsworth.

4. It's good not to be too skeptical because anything is possible.　　　**A　D　N**

5. We can't be certain of anything.　　　**A　D　N**

6. Human behavior is a mysterious thing.　　　**A　D　N**

7. Everything is relative. All ways of "knowing" are equally true.　　　**A　D　N**

8. Scientists/researchers don't know everything.

A D N

9. Some things can't be demonstrated scientifically.

A D N

10. Take action about problems now. There simply isn't time to study them scientifically and fiddle while Rome burns.

A D N

11. Trying to measure client outcome dehumanizes clients, reducing them to the status of a laboratory rat.

A D N

12. Scientific reasoning and data are of no value in planning social policy and social action.

A D N

13. Science is a way of thinking developed by white, male, Western Europeans. It doesn't apply to other cultures.

A D N

SCORE   *Your instructor will provide scoring instructions.*

1. Imagine one type of practitioner who agrees with your instructor's suggested answers and reasons for Exercise 2 and another who does not agree. Which type would do the least harm to clients? Why?

_____

_____

_____

_____

_____

_____

_____

2. Which type would most likely help clients? Why?

_____

_____

_____

_____

_____

_____

_____

2 RECOGNIZING PROPAGANDA IN HUMAN-SERVICES ADVERTISING
The importance of questioning claims about what helps clients

Slick emotional appeals can block critical thinking about any subject. Most people are somewhat skeptical about advertisements that appear in the popular press and on television. Such advertisements use various emotional appeals and arguments to promise all kinds of things: Buy this product and a lush growth of hair will sprout thickly like a rug on your head. If you're over sixty, take these pills, and you'll leap around like a kid again. Dab a bit of this scent behind your ears, and attractive people will smile at you and want to nuzzle you. Buy this washing machine and your maintenance worries are over. If only a few people fell for simplistic emotional appeals and arguments, then advertisers couldn't justify spending billions on advertisements.

SOCIAL WORKERS MAKE VITAL DECISIONS

It is one thing for people to spend a few dollars on products that they may not need or that will not meet their expectations, quite another for professionals to base practice decisions on emotional appeals. Social workers make some of the most life-affecting decisions of any profession. A 1991 survey of members of the National Association of Social Workers (NASW) shows that members of NASW are employed in the following specialties: mental health (32.7%), child welfare (16.3%), health care (12.5%), family services (11.3%), school social work (4.7%), substance abuse (4.6%), geriatrics (4.5%), and developmental disabilities (2.7%) (Gibelman & Schervish, 1993, p. 79). Among all professions providing counseling in mental health agencies, social workers occupy the most staff positions (social workers, 36%; nurses, 24%; and psychologists, 16% (Barnett, 1986, p. 5).

Among all of the areas of specialization above, the National Association of Social Workers' Standards (1991, 1987, p. 6) describe the following kinds of decisions made by practitioners: (1) discharge planning for clients in health-care settings, (2) determining which mediation methods will most reduce obstacles to communication and will best address the needs of the divorced and postdivorced in child and elderly custody disputes, (3) screening clients for high-risk factors and determining which methods (e.g., individual, family, group) will best resolve problems, (4) determining which persons are suitable as foster and adoptive parents and whose parental rights should be terminated, and (5) deciding which procedures will best help residents of nursing homes and other long-term-care facilities to experience the best quality of life.

Even medical journals use examples from social work to illustrate knotty decisions about whether to leave children in the home of their biological parents at some risk to them (the risk of a false negative for reabuse) or to remove the child from their home and risk damaging a functioning family (the risk of a false positive for reabuse) (Pettit, 1993). Because social workers make such life-affecting decisions, clients deserve the benefits of well-reasoned decisions, not ones based on emotional and oversimplified arguments.

GOOD INTENTIONS DO NOT INSURE GOOD RESULTS

Whole books have been written documenting the unanticipated harmful effects from efforts intended to help clients (Breggin, 1991; Morgan, 1983). In all professions, sincere efforts to help can result in harm. Consider the efforts of Blenkner, Bloom, and Nielsen (1971) to help the "mentally impaired aged living within the communities outside of institutional walls" (p. 483). They offered intensive social casework to a sample of the aged in the Cleveland area. They hired four experienced social workers with master's degrees and instructed them to: "Do or get others to do, whatever is necessary to meet the needs of the situation" (p. 489). Their intensive services included "financial assistance, medical evaluation, psychiatric consultation, legal consultation, fiduciary and guardianship services, home aide and other home help services, nursing consultation and evaluation, and placement in a protective setting" (p. 489). During a year of intensive helping, the four caseworkers conducted 2,421 personal casework interviews with 76 aged persons and their helpers (an average of 31.8 interviews per participant).

At the end of the demonstration year, the death rate for clients in the intensive treatment group was 25%; the death rate in the control group was 18%! How could this be? It turned out that the social workers in the treated group had relocated 34% of their clients to nursing homes, while only 20% of clients in the control group were relocated. The researchers concluded that relocation stressed their aged clients. (For critiques of this study and replies to them, see Berger & Piliavin, 1976; Fischer & Hudson, 1976.)

The point of this example is that the best of intentions, the sincerest wishes to do good, the most well-meaning of purposes do not insure good results. Furthermore, had Blenkner, et al., relied purely on their emotions and impressions, deciding not to record and analyze data about the death rate, they would never have known they were doing harm.

HOW EMOTIONAL ARGUMENTS CAN HARM

Any argument that uses emotional appeals to get you to adopt a method without careful, analytical, critical, scientific, data-based thinking could result in decisions that harm rather than help clients. Learning how to avoid accepting an argument by being sucked into its emotional appeal is a vital step in learning to think critically. In your role as practitioner, you face a situation analogous to that of Odysseus, a character in Greek mythology, who had to guide his ship past the treacherous sirens' song. Odysseus was forewarned that the sirens' song was so seductive that any captain or crew who heard it would be lured straight to a reef, where the ship would strike and all would drown. Odysseus put wax in his crew's ears so they couldn't hear the sirens' song, but he had them chain him to the mast so that he could hear it but not take over the helm and steer the ship toward the sirens and the reef. As a practitioner, you must steer a course toward effective methods while avoiding the sirens of emotion that could lead you to choose harmful or ineffective methods.

PROPAGANDA

Either propaganda or reasoned inquiry could persuade someone to act in a given way or to believe a given claim. Here is an example of reliance on reasoned judgments: An instructor examines research about the relative effectiveness of eighteen modes of counseling. This analysis includes a summary of 475 studies and 1,761 treatment-effect-size calculations (Glass & Kliegel, 1983). This analysis indicates that behavioral methods were among the most effective. The instructor shows a student this evidence and recommends that the student take a course on behavioral methods next semester.

Propaganda, on the other hand, can be defined as encouraging beliefs or actions with the least thought possible (Ellul, 1965). It refers to deliberate and systematic efforts to influence perceptions, alter thoughts, and influence behavior to achieve aims valued by propagandists (Jowett & O'Donnell, 1992). Propaganda is one-sided. Many advertisements that encourage practitioners to use particular methods fit this definition. Advertisers set out in a deliberate, premeditated, intentional way to influence the beliefs and actions of service providers (e.g., refer clients to a given treatment; pay for a certain kind of training in how to apply a given method; buy an assessment tool such as an anatomically correct doll). Profit may be a key motive in human service advertisements. Although a concern for profit is not incompatible with truthful accounts, advertising generally avoids giving data and arguments pro and con. Most advertisements do not present any evidence to support the advertised methods (such evidence may or may not be available), but instead appeal to the readers'/viewers' emotions.

To avoid being taken in, you can watch for the following:

1. Always keep in mind the central questions: What conclusion does the material/person want me to accept? What kind of evidence is presented in support of that argument? Typically, the bottom line in professional contexts is whether a given method really helps clients remove complaints.

2. Be aware of emotional appeals in the media, such as a strikingly attractive person, background music to set a mood, or a pleasant or shocking setting in which the argument is presented.

3. Keep in mind that editors can edit material (text, film, video) to support favored views. For example, they may juxtapose events to suggest a causal relationship and include only material that supports a given mood or conclusion.

4. Beware of the style of presentation, including the presenter's apparent sincerity, which suggests a valid belief that the treatment method works; the fluid ease of a well-prepared presentation, which supports confidence in the conclusion; the presenter's attempts to appear similar to the audience; and the use of anecdotes and humor that entertain but do not inform.

5. Beware of the effect of the presenter's status on the audience: degrees and titles (e.g., professor, doctor, MSW, RN), affiliations with organizations familiar to the audience, favorable introduction by someone familiar to us.

6. Keep in mind the following hierarchy, from least to most informative:

   - Anecdotes and stories
   - Experience with a single case; experience with a lot of cases
   - Experience with a single case where clearly defined outcomes have been measured before and after intervention
   - Single-subject designs that involve repeated measures over different phases (e.g., baseline and intervention)
   - Pre–post group designs that do not involve random assignment
   - Multiple-baseline designs
   - Group designs in which subjects are randomly assigned to different treatments or to a treatment and a control group
   - Replicated randomized controlled experiments
   - Replicated randomized controlled experiments that evaluate client-by-treatment interactions

Human service advertisements that rely on simplistic emotional appeals tend to have the following general features:

1. They involve persons of status, who probably sincerely believe in a given program and argue that the method works but do not cite critical tests or claims.

2. The presentation is well rehearsed and smooth, relying on style, not evidence, to support its points.

3. The presentation relies heavily on visual and auditory images to lull the audience into not asking questions about whether or not the method works.

4. The presentation presents only one side of an argument, never referring to evidence that the program is ineffective or might do harm.

5. The presentation often relies on common fallacies, for example, testimonials (statements by those who claim to have been helped by the method) and case examples (detailed descriptions of

individual cases that supposedly represent the client population that has benefitted from the treatment).

You will learn more about fallacies later in this workbook.

ABOUT THE EXERCISES   Learning to think critically requires practice. Consequently, the three exercises in Part 2 use videotaped examples to demonstrate emotional and simplistic arguments in human-service advertising, professional conferences, and the media. You will probably view a videotape, then respond to the corresponding exercise in the Workbook. Exercise 3 demonstrates the characteristics of human-service advertisements. It asks you to view a videotape of claims, then evaluate what you have seen on a form designed to identify advertisements. Exercise 4 presents a classic videotape of a presentation by Dr. Myron L. Fox. A questionnaire and an article explain further what the Dr. Fox exercise is about. In Exercise 5, you will view and think about a widely aired television special about the Juvenile Awareness Program at Rahway Prison in New Jersey.

We recommend that you carefully follow your instructor's suggestions for completing exercises. Some instructors may want you to see this section only *after* you have reacted to videotaped material. Others may want you to read about each exercise *before* you see the videotapes.

Exercise 3
EVALUATING HUMAN-SERVICES ADVERTISEMENTS

PURPOSE

1. To demonstrate what health and human-services advertisements look like.
2. To increase your skills in recognizing weak appeals.

BACKGROUND

Human-services advertisements are claims made by organizations or individuals offering a service or treatment through media (e.g., printed handbills, videotapes, films, audiotapes, videodiscs) to encourage professionals and/or potential clients to use the service without presenting any evidence that the service is effective in achieving the outcomes promised (e.g., an evaluation study, a quasi-experimental study, or a reference to studies evaluating the service), or presenting survey data to support any generalizations made about clients. Emotions, rather than data, are appealed to. Advertisements present only the positives. They do not refer to counterevidence, and they tend to ignore or oversimplify complex issues.

In your area, there are probably various groups of practitioners, hospitals, and organizations that advertise their programs. The large, progressive organizations may produce promotional videos. Professional journals, including *Social Work,* contain full-page advertisements. Half-hour promotional television programs advertise weight loss, study skills, smoking cessation, and other types of self-help programs. Often, professional conferences include presentations that have the criteria for an advertisement: A charismatic, well-known person describes a treatment method, presents the method in a charismatic and entertaining way, and does not raise the issue of effectiveness.

Your instructor may choose to use a videotape from Rogers Memorial Hospital, in Oconomowok, Wisconsin. It speaks highly of administrators and staff at Rogers Hospital that they allowed us to use their videotape in this exercise, as they knew we would critically analyze it. They said they did this because they are committed to professional education.

INSTRUCTIONS

1. Watch the videotape.
2. Answer the questions on the Human-Services Advertisement Spotting Form on pages 49–50 (Exhibit 3.1).

Exhibit 3.1   **HUMAN-SERVICES ADVERTISEMENT SPOTTING FORM**

Your Name   Date

Course

Instructor's Name

Please answer the following questions by circling your responses and by noting your reasons in the space below each statement.

The presentation . . .

1. Argued that some form of treatment or intervention works.   **YES   NO**

2. Gave data or measures of outcome (i.e., figures based on an evaluation study involving relevant outcome measures and random assignment of clients to different groups to determine if the program works).   **YES   NO**

3. Presented testimonials as evidence (testimonials are statements by those who claim to have been helped by a program).   **YES   NO**

4. Appealed to your emotions (e.g., sympathy, fear, anger) as a major persuasive tactic. Such appeals may include music or strikingly attractive or unattractive people and/or locations.   **YES   NO**

5. Presented case examples as evidence (e.g., a professional describes or shows in detail what went on in the treatment and how the client responded.	**YES**	**NO**
6. Mentioned the possibility of harmful (iatrogenic) effects of the treatment.	**YES**	**NO**
7. Presented evidence for and against the use of the program.	**YES**	**NO**
8. Was presented by a speaker whose presentation and manner was extremely well rehearsed, smooth, polished, and attractive.	**YES**	**NO**
9. Was presented by a well-known person or a person of high status, implying that the claim of treatment effectiveness is true because this high-status person says it is.	**YES**	**NO**
10. Encouraged you to think carefully about the effectiveness of the method before referring clients to it.	**YES**	**NO**

SCORE   *Your instructor will provide scoring instructions.*

1. Rank (1982, p. 147) has identified five features of advertising:
   - *Attention Getting:* physically (visual images, lighting, sound) and emotionally (words and images with strong emotional associations)
   - *Confidence Building:* establishing trust by stating that you should believe the expert because he or she is sincere and has good intentions
   - *Desire Stimulating:* the pleasure to be gained, the pain to be avoided, the problem solved. This is the main selling point as to why one should buy the idea or product.
   - *Urgency Stressing:* the encouragement to act now to avoid problems later—to act before it is too late. Advertising that utilizes this approach is often called the "hard" sell; that which does not is a "soft" sell. Urgency stressing is common but not universal to all advertising.
   - *Response Seeking:* trying to learn if the advertisement worked, if the product was bought, if the customer acted in some way desired by the advertiser.

   According to the form on pp. 49–50, which human-service advertisement features does the Rogers Hospital video demonstrate?

   _____

   _____

   _____

   _____

   _____

2. Why do you think these features were used?

   _____

   _____

   _____

   _____

   _____

   _____

   _____

   _____

Exercise 4
WATCHING DOCTOR FOX

PURPOSE

To be learned as you do the exercise.

BACKGROUND

This exercise depends on the Dr. Fox videotape. Please forgive its quality. The videotape was recorded in the late 1960s and has been carefully copied for the Workbook by Dr. Donald H. Naftulin, a medical educator and researcher. Typically, the lecture has been presented live or on videotape to professional audiences at teacher training conferences, at meetings of professional counselors, and in graduate-level university courses. Dr. Fox's audiences have included psychiatrists, psychologists, social-work educators, psychiatric social workers, and other educators and administrators (Naftulin, Ware, & Donnelly, 1973). Unfortunately, the videotape does not include Dr. Myron Fox's introduction, but he was introduced to his audiences with an impressive list of qualifications regarding his knowledge about the applications of mathematics to human behavior. The topic of the videotape is "Game Theory as Applied to Physician Education" (p. 631).

INSTRUCTIONS

We recommend that you *do not skim this exercise* or read ahead unless your instructor gives specific instructions otherwise. *Read only the Instructions section.* Then do the exercise, step by step, in order.

1. Watch the Dr. Fox videotape.
2. Complete the items on the Dr. Fox Questionnaire (Exhibit 4.1).

    Stop here unless directed otherwise!

3. Read the article (Exhibit 4.2).

Exhibit 4.1 **DOCTOR FOX QUESTIONNAIRE**

Your Name   Date

Course

Instructor's Name

Please circle one response to each item below.

1.	Did the speaker seem interested in his subject?	**YES**	**NO**
2.	Did he dwell on the obvious?	**YES**	**NO**
3.	Did he use enough examples to clarify his material?	**YES**	**NO**
4.	Did he present his material in a well-organized form?	**YES**	**NO**
5.	Did he stimulate your thinking?	**YES**	**NO**
6.	Did he present his materials in an interesting way?	**YES**	**NO**
7.	Have you read any of this speaker's publications?	**YES**	**NO**

8. Did the speaker appear well informed about his topic? **YES** **NO**

9. Did the speaker present ideas that may be potentially useful to human-services practitioners? **YES** **NO**

10. Did the speaker present ideas that may be potentially useful to psychiatrists? **YES** **NO**

11. Describe any other important characteristics of his presentation.

_____

_____

_____

_____

_____

_____

_____

_____

_____

_____

_____

_____

_____

SCORE *Your instructor will provide scoring instructions.*

After you complete the Doctor Fox Questionnaire, read the article beginning on the next page, "The Doctor Fox Lecture: A Paradigm of Educational Seduction." The article explains that none of the professionals who watched the lecture in person, or who saw it on videotape, detected the lecture for what it was—filled with contradictions, nonsequiturs, vagueness, glittering generalizations, neologisms—some would say nonsense!

Exhibit 4.2

THE DOCTOR FOX LECTURE:
A PARADIGM OF EDUCATIONAL SEDUCTION

Donald H. Naftulin, M.D., John E. Ware, Jr.,
and Frank A. Donnelly

Abstract—On the basis of publications supporting the hypothesis that student ratings of educators depend largely on personality variables and not educational content, the authors programmed an actor to teach charismatically and nonsubstantively on a topic about which he knew nothing. The authors hypothesized that given a sufficiently impressive lecture paradigm, even experienced educators participating in a new learning experience can be seduced into feeling satisfied that they have learned despite irrelevant, conflicting, and meaningless content conveyed by the lecturer. The hypothesis was supported when 55 subjects responded favorably at the significant level to an eight-item questionnaire concerning their attitudes toward the lecture. The study serves as an example to educators that their effectiveness must be evaluated beyond the satisfaction with which students view them and raises the possibility of training actors to give "legitimate" lectures as an innovative approach toward effective education. The authors conclude by emphasizing that student satisfaction with learning may represent little more than the illusion of having learned.

Teaching effectiveness is difficult to study since so many variables must be considered in its evaluation. Among the obvious are the education, social background, knowledge of subject matter, experience, and personality of the educator. It would seem that an educator with the proper combination of these and other variables would be effective. However, such a combination may result in little more than the educator's ability to satisfy students, but not necessarily educate them.

Getzels and Jackson (1) have stated that the personality of the teacher might be the most significant variable in the evaluation of teaching effectiveness. Wallen and Travers (1) also supported this concept in stating that "we have tried to demonstrate that patterns of teacher behavior and the teaching methods they represent are mainly the products of forces which have little to do with scientific knowledge of learning."

Similarly, Goffman (2) viewed audience receptivity to a lecturer as highly influenced by the person introducing him as well as by the quality of the introduction. In addition, Goffman described an audience as influenced by the speaker's "involuntary expressive behavior" as much as by the expressed information he wished to convey. This is especially so if the audience has had little time to evaluate the information. Consequently, the learner's impression of the information conveyer becomes a decisive factor in how he responds to the information conveyed.

Rogers (3) stressed the importance of humanizing our educational institutions by bringing "together the cognitive and the affective-experiential" aspects of learning. He also discussed the significance of the educator's genuineness. He feels that the educator who does not present a facade is more likely to be effective. The educator, states Rogers,

This article is based on a paper presented at the 11th Annual Conference on Research in Medical Education at the 83rd Annual Meeting of the AAMC, Miami Beach, Florida, November 6, 1972.

Dr. Naftulin is associate professor and director of the Division of Continuing Education in Psychiatry, University of Southern California School of Medicine; Mr. Ware is assistant professor of medical education and health care planning and director of research and evaluation, Southern Illinois University School of Medicine; Mr. Donnelly is an instructor in psychiatry (psychology) in the USC Division of Continuing Education in Psychiatry.

must have a "direct personal encounter with the learner."

In one study (4) in which student perceptions of educators in 1,427 seventh through 12th grade classes were factor analyzed, it was reported that the students regarded "teacher charisma or popularity" as the most important characteristic when rating teachers. The article further states that "students do not respond directly to specific questions regarding teacher effectiveness. Rather a kind of halo effect on teacher charisma or popularity determines to a large extent how students react to questions about their teacher."

If charisma or popularity have such an effect on the rating of teachers by junior high and high school students, the authors wondered whether the ratings of a highly trained group of professional educators in a learning situation might be similarly influenced. If that were the case, a demonstration of the personality factor in perceived learning might serve to arouse the group members' concern about the proper combination of style and substance in their own teaching.

METHOD

The hypothesis for this study was as follows. Given a sufficiently impressive lecture paradigm, an experienced group of educators participating in a new learning situation can feel satisfied that they have learned despite irrelevant, conflicting, and meaningless content conveyed by the lecturer. To test the hypothesis, the authors selected a professional actor who looked distinguished and sounded authoritative; provided him with a sufficiently ambiguous title, Dr. Myron L. Fox, an authority on the application of mathematics to human behavior; dressed him up with a fictitious but impressive curriculum vitae, and presented him to a group of highly trained educators.

The lecture method was the teaching format selected since it is one used extensively in the professional educational setting. It has been described as the one teaching method during which most of the time the instructor talks to the students (1). Its acceptance as an effective teaching tool is attributable mainly to its time-testedness.

Dr. Fox's topic was to be "Mathematical Game Theory as Applied to Physician Education." His source material was derived from a complex but sufficiently understandable scientific article geared to lay readers (5). One of the authors, on two separate occasions, coached the lecturer to present his topic and conduct his question and answer period with an excessive use of double talk, neologisms, non sequiturs, and contradictory statements. All this was to be interspersed with parenthetical humor and meaningless references to unrelated topics.

GROUP I

Eleven psychiatrists, psychologists, and social-worker educators who were gathered for a teacher training conference in continuing education comprised the learner group. The purpose of the conference was to help this group be more effective educators of other health professionals by providing them various instructional goals, media, and experiences. Dr. Fox was introduced as "the real McCoy" to this unsuspecting group; and he presented his one-hour lecture in the manner described, followed by a half hour discussion period which was hardly more substantive.

At the end of his performance an authentic looking satisfaction questionnaire was distributed to which all 11 mental health educators were asked to respond anonymously (Table 1). The introduction of the lecturer as well as his lecture and discussion were videotaped for use with other groups.

Significantly, more favorable than unfavorable responses to the questionnaire were obtained (chi-square = 35.96, $p < .001$). The one item with most favorable responses was the first, "Did he dwell upon the obvious?" It was the feeling of half the group that he did. The remaining items received a majority of favorable responses. No respondent reported having read Dr. Fox's publications. Subjective responses included the following:

> Excellent presentation, enjoyed listening. Has warm manner. Good flow, seems enthusiastic. What about the two types of games, zero-sum and non-zero sum? Too intellectual a presentation. My orientation is more pragmatic.

Because the first group was few in number and quite select, the authors sought other subjects with similar experience and professional identity who might provide further data to test the hypothesis.

GROUP II

The second group consisted of 11 subjects who were psychiatrists, psychologists, and psychiatric social workers, all identified as mental health educators. A videotape of the previously described lecture and discussion period as well as the preparatory introduction was shown to the group.

Table 1
Examples of Questions Used and Percentage of Responses*
for Three Groups

Questions	Group I Yes	Group I No	Group II Yes	Group II No	Group III Yes	Group III No
Did he dwell upon the obvious?	50	50	0	100	28	72
Did he seem interested in his subject?	100	0	91	9	97	3
Did he use enough examples to clarify his material?	90	10	64	36	91	9
Did he present his material in a well organized form?	90	10	82	18	70	30
Did he stimulate your thinking?	100	0	91	9	87	13
Did he put his material across in an interesting way?	90	10	82	18	81	19
Have you read any of this speaker's publications?	0	100	9	91	0	100
Specify any other important characteristics of his presentation.						

*"Yes" responses to all but item one are considered favorable.

After the presentation group members responded to it using the same questionnaire as did the first group (Table 1). Favorable responses far outweighed unfavorable responses, and the difference between the two was (chi square = 64.53, $p <$ .001). All responded favorably to the first item, which means that they felt he did not "dwell upon the obvious." There were also significantly more favorable than unfavorable responses to the other items and one respondent reported having read the lecturer's publications. Some subjective statements were:

> Did not carry it far enough. Lack of visual materials to relate it to psychiatry. Too much gesturing. Left out relevant examples. He misses the last few phrases which I believe would have tied together his ideas for me.

Still more subjects were sought to further test the hypothesis.

GROUP III

The third group was different in that it consisted of 33 educators and administrators enrolled in a graduate level university educational philosophy course. Of the 33 subjects in this group, 21 held master's degrees, eight had bachelor's degrees, and four had other degrees which were not specified. Most of these educators were not specifically mental health professionals but had been identified as having counseling experience in their respective schools. The videotape of the lecture was again presented to this group, after which the educators responded to it by using the same questionnaire as the first two groups (Table 1).

Again the number of favorable responses was significantly greater than the number of unfavorable responses (chi square = 102.83, $p <$ .001). The majority of respondents from Group III also did not feel the lecturer dwelt upon the obvious, and they also responded favorably for the most part to the other items. Subjective responses, when given, were again interesting. Some were:

> Lively examples. His relaxed manner of presentation was a large factor in holding my interest. Extremely articulate. Interesting, wish he dwelled more on background. Good analysis of subject that has been personally studied before. Very dramatic presentation. He was certainly captivating. Somewhat disorganized. Frustratingly boring. Unorganized and ineffective. Articulate. Knowledgeable.

Given the responses of these three groups of educators to the lecture paradigm, the authors believe that the study hypothesis has been supported.

DISCUSSION

The notion that students, even if they are professional educators, can be effectively "seduced" into an illusion of having learned if the lecturer simulates a style of authority and wit is certainly not new. In a terse but appropriate statement on educators, Postman and Weingartner (6) emphasized that "it is the sign of a competent crap detector that he is not completely captivated by the arbitrary abstractions of the community in which he happened to grow up." The three groups of learners in this study, all of whom had grown up in the academic community and were experienced educators, obvious failed as "competent crap detectors" and were seduced by the style of Dr. Fox's presentation. Considering the educational sophistication of the subjects, it is striking that none of them detected the lecture for what it was.

In addition to testing the hypothesis, the paradigm was to provide these professional educators with an example of being educationally seduced and to demonstrate that there is much more to teaching than making students happy. A balanced combination of knowledge and personality are needed for effective teaching even if the student does not require the former to sustain the illusion that he has learned. It is hoped that this experience has helped respondents from these three groups to question their educational effectiveness more meaningfully.

To the authors' knowledge a simulated teaching paradigm such as this with student responses to subsequently perceived learning has not been reported. Despite the usual reservations about generalizing data from only 55 subjects, the results of the study raise some interesting questions. The first involves the content of the lecture. Does a topic seemingly short on content and long on ambiguity or abstraction lend itself more readily to such a lecture paradigm than a content-based factual presentation from a more concrete topic area? The answer is an equivocal "yes," as a subject in Group I noted after being told of the study's design. He said he felt that the lecturer might have had a tougher time talking nonsense about a more concrete topic but even under those circumstances a fake lecture could be "pulled off" with an unsuspecting group. This raises the next question.

If the group were more sophisticated about a more concrete aspect of the lecturer's subject matter, in this case mathematics, would he have been as successful in seducing the respondents into an illusion of having learned? Probably not. Or at least the lecturer would have to be extremely skillful to be successful. The study also raises the larger issue of what mix of style and substance in the lecture method is optimal for not just integrating information in a meaningful way but for providing learning motivation as well. Although the study was not specifically addressed to this question, the fact that no respondents saw through the hoax of the lecture, that all respondents had significantly more favorable than unfavorable responses, and that one even believed he read Dr. Fox's publications suggests that for these learners "style" was more influential than "content" in providing learner satisfaction.

A more ideal assessment of the relative value of content and style in determining learner-reporter satisfaction might consist of programming the same "lecturer" to systematically alter the content of his presentation before three equivalent groups of learners. Simultaneously, his "involuntary expressive behavior" would remain constant for each of the three groups; for example, Group A would receive sufficient content conveyed with sufficient "involuntary expressive behavior," Group B moderately insufficient content accompanied by the same "involuntary expressive behavior" as was displayed with Group A, and Group C totally inadequate content delivered in the same manner as to the first two groups; the three groups of learners could then be more systematically compared as to learner perceived satisfaction.

After the respondents in the actual study were informed of its purpose, numerous subjects from each group requested the article from which the lecturer was programmed. Reported intent of these requests ranged from curiosity to disbelief, but the authors were told by some respondents that Dr. Fox did stimulate interest in the subject area even after the respondents were told of the study's purpose. Despite having been misinformed, the motivation of some respondents to learn more about the subject matter persisted. Consequently, it is the authors' impression that the "arbitrary abstractions" suggested by Postman and Weingartner have some initial pump-priming effect on educational motivation.

The relationship of the illusion of having learned to motivation for learning more has not been fully addressed here, but should a positive relationship exist, this study supports the possibility of training actors to give legitimate lectures as an innovative educational approach toward student-perceived satisfaction with the learning process. The corollary would be to provide the scholar-educator with a more dramatic stage presence to enhance student satisfaction with the learning process. Either extreme has a soap-selling quality not likely to lather the enthusiasm of the pure scholar. However, this paper is not addressed to him but rather to student-perceived satisfaction with how well he has shared his information. More important, as has been noted, it suggests to the educator that the extent to which his students are satisfied with his teaching, and even the degree to which they feel they have learned, reflects little more than their illusions of having learned.

REFERENCES

1. Gage, N. L. (Ed.). *Handbook of Research on Teaching*. New York: Rand McNally, 1963, pp. 506, 464, and 481.
2. Goffman, E. *The Presentation of Self in Everyday Life*. New York: Doubleday, 1959.
3. Rogers, C. R. Bringing Together Ideas and Feelings in Learning. *Learning Today*, 5:32–43, Spring, 1972.
4. Coats, W. D., and Swierenga, L. Student Perceptions of Teachers. A Factor Analytic Study. *J. Educ. Res.*, 65:357–360, April, 1972.
5. Rapoport, A. The Use and Misuse of Game Theory. *Scientific American*, 207:108–114, December, 1962.
6. Postman, N., and Weingartner, C. *Teaching as a Subversive Activity*. New York: Delacorte Press, 1969, pp. 1–15.

DISCUSSION

The article you just read has sparked interest because several much more methodologically sophisticated studies have replicated the Dr. Fox effect. In one study, 207 students were randomly assigned to high or low seduction and high or low content conditions; then, they rated the presented material (Ware & Williams, 1975). Another study involving 161 students followed essentially the same design (Meier & Feldhusen, 1979). In both studies, the instructor's expressive and seductive style accounted for higher student ratings. Apparently, style of presentation can emerge victorious over content when students rate their instruction.

Other studies seem to indicate that, though style of presentation greatly influences how students rated their instruction, other variables, such as whether students have a chance to study and whether incentives are provided for accurate knowledge, influence ratings (Perry, Abrami, & Leventhal, 1979). A recent review concluded, "In the condition most like the university classroom, where students were told before viewing the lecture that they would be tested on the materials and that they would be rewarded in accordance with the number of exam questions which they answered correctly . . . the Dr. Fox effect was not supported" (Marsh, 1987, p. 332).

In summary, we think the research supports the conclusion that many professional conferences present ideal conditions for Dr. Fox: The audience is exposed only once to a short speech, the audience expects to be entertained, and the audience will not be rated on its ability to master the content of the speech. The extent to which the Dr. Fox effect influences student ratings of faculty at the end of the academic year remains unclear, but students should consider carefully that they may rate their teachers more on their style or charisma, less on how well they taught thinking skills.

FOLLOW-UP QUESTIONS

1. How did you score on the Doctor Fox Questionnaire? Why?

_____

_____

_____

2. What techniques did Dr. Fox use to seduce his audience into thinking that he had given an instructive lecture?

_____

_____

_____

3. Why do you think none of the fifty-five professionals who saw the lecture detected the ruse?

_____

_____

_____

4. If this lecture were updated and presented at a professional conference today, what proportion of the audience do you think would detect the ruse? Why do you think so?

_____

_____

_____

5. How would you prepare yourself to avoid being taken in by a seductive presentation?

_____

_____

_____

6. Do you think students rate instructors based on the instructor's style of presentation?

_____

_____

_____

7. How can educators prepare human service workers to become "competent crap detectors" (Naftulin, et al., 1973, p. 633)?

_____

_____

_____

Exercise 5

DOES SCARING YOUTH HELP THEM "GO STRAIGHT"?

Applying Principles of Reasoning, Inference, Decision Making, and Evaluation (PRIDE 1)

PURPOSE

To be learned as you do the exercise.

BACKGROUND

The Juvenile Awareness Program at Rhaway Prison in New Jersey has served as a model for more than fifty similar programs to follow it. The program is run by the Lifers, who are inmates who currently serve a life sentence. The program is intended to prevent delinquency.

INSTRUCTIONS

1. View and take notes on the videotape.
2. In the fifteen minutes following the videotape, read the situation presented in Exhibit 5.1, then record your answers to the three questions about the case material in "Scared Straight." You may use one of the pieces of paper that accompany this exercise for your notes; the other is for your answer to three questions below. Please write clearly.

Exhibit 5.1   **"Scared Straight"**

Your Name _____   Date _____

Course _____

Instructor's Name _____

Situation   *Assume that you have taken a job as a probation-parole officer working with juvenile clients who are adjudicated by a local juvenile court. Your supervisor at your agency has asked you to view this audiovisual material and to suggest whether juveniles, who are served by your probation-parole agency, should participate in a program like the one in "Scared Straight."*

1. What is the one central conclusion that the makers of "Scared Straight" would have you draw regarding the Juvenile Awareness Program? (List the *one* major conclusion below.)

    _____

    _____

    _____

    _____

    _____

2. Would you, based purely on what you see in   **Yes   No**
    this audiovisual material about the "Scared
    Straight" program, recommend that your
    agency try such a program with its clients?
    (Circle one.)

3. Why would you or would you not recommend that a "Scared Straight" program be tried on your agency's clients? (Please explain your answer to Question 2.)

_____

_____

_____

_____

_____

_____

_____

_____

_____

_____

_____

_____

_____

_____

_____

_____

_____

_____

_____

_____

_____

_____

_____

_____

SCORE   *Your instructor will provide scoring instructions.*

Exhibit 5.2

FOLLOW-UP QUESTIONS

1. What was your score?

2. What is the dominant form of evidence in the "Scared Straight"
    film or videotape?

3. Why did you respond as you did to the highly emotional
    argument in the "Scared Straight" film or videotape?

4. Do you think the Juvenile Awareness Program might have produced harmful effects on juveniles?

_____

_____

_____

5. Is this measure a valid test of critical-thinking? Explain your answer.

_____

_____

_____

_____

_____

_____

_____

_____

_____

_____

_____

_____

_____

_____

_____

_____

_____

3 FALLACIES AND PITFALLS IN PROFESSIONAL DECISION MAKING

What they are and how to avoid them

How you think about your practice affects the quality of services clients receive. Let's say you attend a conference to learn about a new method for helping clients, and the presenter appeals to the audience by saying that you should adopt the method because it is new. Would that be sufficient grounds to adopt the method? What if the presenter described in detail a few clients who had been helped by the method, or had a few clients describe their own successful experiences with it? Would you then use the method? Let's say that when staff who manage a refuge for battered women test residents' self-esteem, both before and after residents participate in a support group, they find that the women score higher after taking part in the support group. Can we assume that the support group caused an increase in residents' self-esteem? Or, what if an interdisciplinary team decides that a child requires special education services. The group's leader encourages the group to come up with a unanimous decision. Can we assume that because none of the participants raised objections that all major evidence and relevant arguments regarding placement have been heard?

Each of these situations represents a potential for error in reasoning about practice. In the first, the presenter encourages acceptance of a method because it is new (appeal to newness), by describing a few selected instances (reliance on case examples), and offers statements made by a few clients who have been helped by the method (testimonials). In the second, staff at the refuge for battered women assume that because improvement followed treatment, the treatment caused improvement (the post hoc fallacy). The final example concerns a potential problem with group reasoning: Group members may not share dissenting opinions because they fear upsetting group cohesion (groupthink). These fallacies will become clear as you do the exercises in this workbook.

You can learn to avoid common reasoning errors by becoming familiar with them and developing strategies to avoid them. Literature in four major areas can help us to understand practice fallacies: (1) philosophy (especially concerning critical thinking and informal logic), (2) psychology (including relevant social-psychological studies), (3) sociology (especially the study of how problems are defined); and (4) professions such as medicine (studies of clinical reasoning, decision making, and judgment). The five exercises in Part 3 seek to distill this literature into understandable, useful principles and lessons for avoiding practice fallacies. For a warm-up, let's consider a practice situation that illustrates a fallacy.

WARM-UP EXAMPLE IN PRACTICE REASONING

BACKGROUND

A state human-service agency licenses foster homes and places children in them. One worker makes this comment about a co-worker:

> Ms. Beyer forms impressions of potential foster homes very early. Once she forms an impression, she never budges from it. She bases her initial impression on her own housekeeping standards (whether the potential foster home smells and looks clean). She seems to ignore the parent's ability to care for the kids, criminal records, references from others in the community, how the foster parent's own children have adjusted, and so on.

DISCUSSION

What's wrong here? Initial impressions "anchor" all that goes after. No matter what new evidence emerges, the initial impression prevails. This kind of faulty reasoning is called *anchoring and insufficient adjustment*. It gets in the way of discovering helpful data and identifying alternate perspectives that can help you make sound judgments and decisions. Anchoring and insufficient adjustment of initial estimates have been reported in the medical literature as having costly and painful results (Kassirer & Kopelman, 1991).

The exercises in Part 3 offer definitions of other fallacies and pitfalls as well as suggestions for avoiding them. By illustrating each fallacy with case material and by encouraging your active participation in the exercises, we hope you will hone your skills to spot and avoid fallacies in your work with clients.

ABOUT THE EXERCISES

Exercise 6, Using the Professional Thinking Form, is the only exercise in Part 3 that does not require group participation. You could use this to evaluate what you have learned in Part 3 by completing the Professional Thinking Form both before and after Exercises 7–11. In the three Reasoning-in-Practice Games (Exercises 7, 8, and 9), two teams compete. Working in teams allows teammates to learn from each other. The goal of each team is to identify the fallacies in the practice vignettes. Either a narrator in each group reads a vignette aloud or participants act it out. Games last about ninety minutes. If time is limited, you can set a predetermined time limit to end the game or resume the game later. Games A, B, and C concern, respectively, common practice fallacies; faulty reasoning related to group and interpersonal dynamics, and cognitive biases in practice. Each game defines its fallacies and suggests how to avoid them.

Completing Exercises 6–9 paves the way for a Fallacies Film Festival (Exercise 10). In the fallacies festival, you will team up with a partner to develop and act out an original, 30- to 60-second script illustrating *one* fallacy. Vignettes can be videotaped and shown in a "Fallacies Film Festival" to celebrate what you have learned. The vignettes entertain best if actors ham it up, wear outlandish costumes, add props, and humorously overstate practice situations.

Fallacy Spotting in Professional Contexts (Exercise 11) asks you to select an example of fallacious reasoning, quote its source, and explain the fallacy.

We hope that these exercises will help you to use sound reasoning on the job. All the exercises try to bridge the gap between critical thinking and practice by involving you in *doing* something. Although we encourage you to have fun with the exercises, we also ask you to remember that the kinds of decisions involved in the vignettes are serious business. They influence such decisions as which foster homes children will go to, which probationers will walk the streets, which individuals who call a crisis hotline will be helped, which methods will be used to mediate between divorcing parents or to try to prevent drug abuse among school children.

Exercise 6
USING THE PROFESSIONAL THINKING FORM

PURPOSE

1. To test your skill in identifying common practice fallacies.
2. To help you to identify fallacies in reasoning about practice.

BACKGROUND

The Professional Thinking Form (Exhibit 6.1) evaluates your skill in spotting fallacies that cloud thinking in the helping professions. Each of its twenty-five vignettes describes an example of thinking in practice. Some involve a fallacy; others do not. Vignettes include examples of practice decisions related to individuals, families, groups, and communities with various areas including health, mental health, child welfare, chemical dependency, and research.

INSTRUCTIONS

Each situation describes something that you may encounter in practice.

1. Consider each situation from the standpoint of critical, analytical, scientific thinking.
2. In the space provided, write brief responses, as follows:
   a. If an item is objectionable from a critical standpoint, then write a statement that describes what is wrong with it. Items may or may not contain an error in thinking.
   b. If you cannot make up your mind on one, then mark it with a question mark (?), but leave none blank.
   c. If you are satisfied with the item as it stands, then mark it "OK."

Please write your main point(s) as concisely as possible. The form takes about thirty minutes to complete.

Exhibit 6.1   **THE PROFESSIONAL THINKING FORM***
BY LEONARD GIBBS AND JOAN WERNER

Your Name _____   Date _____

Course _____

Instructor's Name _____

SITUATIONS FROM PRACTICE

1. "Did you attend the workshop on strategic family therapy? Marian Steinberg is an excellent speaker, and her presentation was so convincing! She treated everyone in the audience like colleagues. She got the whole audience involved in a family sculpture, and she is such a warm person. I must use her methods with my clients."

_____

_____

_____

_____

_____

_____

_____

_____

_____

_____

_____

_____

*Revised by Leonard Gibbs and Joan Stehle-Werner (School of Nursing, University of Wisconsin-Eau Claire) and adapted from L. Gibbs (1991), *Scientific Reasoning for Social Workers* (New York: Macmillan), pp. 54–59, 274–278.

2. "Have you heard of 'Integrated Case Management'? It's a new procedure designed to serve better the needs of foster children, drug-exposed infants, and teenage parents. This approach has just been devised to integrate social work service, health service, and community resources. You ought to try it."

_____

_____

_____

_____

_____

_____

3. "I know that open adoptions, in which birth parents and adoptive parents know each other's identity and can communicate with each other, works well. I read an article by Siegel (1993) that says it works."

_____

_____

_____

_____

_____

_____

_____

4. "Bill has been a worker at the Dulaney Halfway House for ten years. He presented evidence to the county board that the rate of the residents' aggressive behavior has recently increased. His evidence contradicts the Dulaney Board of Directors' Self-Study Report. Other staff reject Bill's argument because they don't like him. He is a homosexual."

_____

_____

_____

_____

_____

_____

5. "I note that the authors never define the word *codependency* in their article on codependency among people who abuse alcohol. I need a definition of this term before I can understand what is being discussed."

_____

_____

_____

_____

_____

_____

6. "I know Ms. Sanchez has just completed a two-year study with random-assignment control groups and a six-month follow-up to study the effects of treatment for chemical dependency here at Hepworth Treatment Center, but my experience indicates otherwise. My experience here as a counselor has shown me that Ms. Sanchez's results are wrong."

_____

_____

_____

_____

_____

_____

7. Workers from the Bayberry County Guidance Clinic were overheard at lunch as saying, "You mean you don't use provocative therapy? I thought everyone used it by now. Provocative therapy is widely used at this facility. Most of the staff is trained in its use. We have all used it here. You should too."

_____

_____

_____

_____

_____

_____

8. "Dr. Trevor H. Noland has degrees from Harvard, MIT, and Stanford. He has held the prestigious Helms Chair of Human Service Studies for ten years. He has been director of psychiatry departments in three universities and has served as a consultant to the National Institute of Mental Health. His stature supports the truth of his ideas in his book on psychotherapy."

_____

_____

_____

_____

_____

9. "I think that we need to exercise caution when we make judgments that our efforts are truly helping clients. Other possible reasons may account for change. Perhaps people just mature. They may get help from some other source. Maybe they get better simply because they expect to get better."

_____

_____

_____

_____

_____

10. At a professional conference, a colleague leans over to you and whispers in your ear, "I don't understand how anyone could accept an opinion from Ms. Washington. Just look at her. Her hair is unkempt, and her slip is showing. How can we accept an idea from someone who looks like a fugitive from an insane asylum?"

_____

_____

_____

_____

_____

_____

11. A director of an evaluation-research consulting firm was over-heard saying, "We conduct studies for agencies to determine how effective their programs are. We never agree to do an evaluation unless we are sure we can produce positive results."

_____

_____

_____

_____

_____

_____

_____

_____

12. Here is a statement made by an agency supervisor to a colleague: "Michelle is one of the most difficult workers to deal with. I asked her to decide between supporting either nutritional or health-care programs to meet the needs of the elderly here in Dane County. She responded that she needed some time to get evidence to study the matter. She said that there may be other alternatives for our resources. As I see it, there are only two ways to go on this issue."

_____

_____

_____

_____

_____

_____

_____

_____

_____

_____

_____

_____

13. At a professional conference, Dr. McDonald asked a family who had participated in "Strategic Family Therapy" to tell the audience how the method worked for them. The husband said to the audience, "Frankly, I didn't think we had a prayer of saving our marriage. When my wife and I made our first appointment with Dr. McDonald, I thought we would go through the motions of seeing a counselor, and we would get a divorce. But as Dr. McDonald requested, my wife and I brought our thirteen-year-old, David, and our eleven-year-old, Emily, with us to counseling. All of us have been surprised, to say the least, by Dr. McDonald's approach. Instead of engaging in a lot of deep, dark discussions, we do exercises as a family. Last time we were requested to go on a treasure hunt with me as a leader for the hunt. Dr. McDonald's exercises have been fun to do. His exercises teach us about our family system. The methods have really helped us, and I highly recommend them to you."

_____

_____

_____

_____

_____

_____

_____

14. Shortly after the city planners announced their intent to build a vocational training facility, they were deluged with phone calls and letters from angry citizens protesting the plan. Planners were surprised that the whole community opposed the plan so strongly.

_____

_____

_____

_____

_____

_____

_____

_____

15. "Most likely this client is depressed."

_____

_____

_____

_____

_____

_____

_____

_____

16. Joe Armejo is a typical Vietnam-War veteran, like most of the clients we see at the Veterans Administration. At seventeen, he entered the marines, went through his basic training, and then "all hell broke loose," as he tells it: "One day I was home on leave riding around the square in the sun with my 'chick'; the next, I was on a C-130 headed for 'Nam, and the next I was in the dark, stinking jungle. That's a change, man!" Joe served in Vietnam eighteen months, often in combat, with a small unit. Among those in his unit, he lost two close buddies, one whose family he still contacts. After the war, Joe drifted from job to job, seemed unable to form a lasting relationship with a woman, and descended into an alcohol addiction that was so deep, "I just reached up and pulled the whole world down on my head." Joe occasionally encountered counselors, but he never opened up to them—not until he joined a Vietnam-War veterans' group. After six months of weekly visits, Joe began to turn his life around. He got and held a job, and he has been dating the same woman for a while now. Joe's dramatic change is typical of men who join such groups.

_____

_____

_____

_____

_____

_____

_____

_____

_____

_____

17. An interviewer asks the following question: "Will you be able to drive yourself to the hospital weekly and eat without dentures until January 1st?"

_____

_____

_____

_____

_____

_____

_____

18. An interviewer asks a female victim of domestic abuse the following question: "You don't want to stay in a home with a violent wife-beater, do you?"

_____

_____

_____

_____

_____

_____

_____

19. "Electroconvulsive (shock) therapy is the most effective treatment for psychotic depression."

_____

_____

_____

_____

_____

_____

_____

20. "One way of describing 'progress' in clients seeking independence from their families is to assess their gradual increase in
independence from their families."

_____

_____

_____

_____

_____

_____

21. "The effectiveness of our program in family therapy is well
documented. Before families enter treatment, we have them fill
out a Family Adjustment Rating Scale, which has a Cronbach's
alpha reliability of .98 and is validly associated with indices of
sexual adjustment and marital communication. After treatment,
we have family members fill out the Scale again. Statistically
significant improvement in these scores after family therapy
proves that our program is effective."

_____

_____

_____

_____

_____

22. A social worker remarks to a client, "It is extremely difficult to
work with people who have adolescent adjustment reactions.
Adolescents have not had sufficient experience to reality test.
This is why those who work with adolescents use existential and
reality-oriented approaches."

_____

_____

_____

_____

_____

23. Don Jaszewski, a social worker at Parkview Elementary School, administered the Rosenberg Self-Concept Scale to all 100 students in the school's fifth grade. For the ten students who scored lowest on the test, Don designed a special program to raise their self-esteem. All ten participated in a weekly rap session, read materials designed to foster self-acceptance and self-assurance, and saw Don individually at frequent intervals during the academic year. When Don again administered the Rosenberg Self-Concept Scale at the end of the program, he was pleased to note the participants' statistically significant improvement from their pretreatment scores. In fact, Don noted that seven of the ten students in his program scored almost average this time. Because of this evidence, Don urged the school administration to offer his program in the future.

24. Mr. Rasmussen, director of the Regional Alcoholic Rehabilitation Clinic, is proud of his treatment facility's success rate. The clinic draws clients who are usually leading citizens in the area and whose insurance companies are willing to pay premium prices for such treatment. Mr. Rasmussen points out proudly that 75% of those who complete this treatment, according to a valid and reliable survey done by an unbiased consulting group, abstain completely from alcohol during the six months following treatment. In contrast, the same consulting firm reports that alcoholics who complete treatment at a local halfway house for unemployed men have a 30% abstinence rate for the six months after their treatment. Mr. Rasmussen says, "The difference between 75% and 30% cannot be ignored. It is obvious that our clinic's multidisciplinary team and intensive case-by-case treatment are producing better results than those at the halfway house."

25. With help from a noted researcher, the Cree County Social Service Department has developed a screening test for families to identify potential child abusers. Experience with this test in the Cree County School District has shown that, among confirmed abusers who took the test, the result was positive (indicating abuse) for 95% of couples who abused their child within the prior year (sensitivity). Also, among nonabusers the test results were negative (indicating no abuse) for 95% (specificity). Cree County records show that abuse occurs in 3 of 100 families (prevalence rate of 3%) in the Cree County School District. County Social Service Department workers note that the Donohue family tested positive (indicating abuse). They conclude that the Donohue family has a 95% chance that they will abuse their child.

Do you agree with the County Social Service Department's estimate? If not, what is the probability that the Donohue family will abuse their child?

_____

_____

_____

_____

_____

_____

SCORE   *Your instructor will provide scoring instructions.*

_____

FOLLOW-UP QUESTION

Do any of the Professional Thinking Form's situations reflect real situations particularly well? Which one(s)?

_____

_____

_____

_____

_____

_____

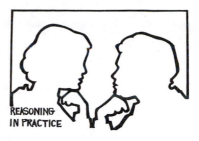

REASONING
IN PRACTICE

THE REASONING-IN-PRACTICE GAMES

PURPOSE

1. To have some fun.
2. To learn how to identify common fallacies or pitfalls related to practice.
3. To learn how to avoid common fallacies related to practice and what countermeasures can be taken.

BACKGROUND

Fallacies are common errors in reasoning. Many fallacies are so common they have their own names; some of them have been recognized for so long that they have Latin names. For example, *ad hominem* means to attack a person rather than critically examining a person's argument. Much has been written about fallacies by those who teach critical thinking (Chaffee, 1988; Damer, 1995; Dowden, 1993; Engel, 1994; Mayfield, 1991; Paul, 1993; Pinto & Blair, 1993; Thouless, 1974). This workbook focuses on how to spot fallacies that occur in practice-related situations. Fallacies about practice are called practitioners' fallacies, or pitfalls in reasoning about practice. Because merely knowing about such fallacies or pitfalls may not help you to avoid them (Fischhoff, 1977; Kurtz & Garfield, 1978; Wood, 1978), we have developed Reasoning-in-Practice Games to engage you actively in spotting, defining, and countering fallacies. The fallacies in Game A (Common Practice Fallacies) are grouped together because they are possibly the most universal and deceptive. Many involve selective attention or partiality in using evidence (e.g., case example, testimonial, focusing only on successes). Those in Game B (Group and Interpersonal Dynamics) describe fallacies that often occur in task groups, committees, and agency politics. Additional sources of error are illustrated in Game C (Cognitive Biases in Practice), which draws on research about judgments and decision making in psychology and other helping professions.

GENERAL INSTRUCTIONS FOR GAMES A, B, AND C

Please read these general instructions before doing Exercises 7–9.

1. Read the Definitions section for the game you want to play. Study the definitions for about one hour. By doing this, you will get the most from the game. Imagine how the fallacy and its countermeasures might apply to your clients and to your work with fellow professionals.

   Most vignettes depict just one fallacy. We hope that your active participation, the realistic vignettes, and the immediate feedback will help you learn critical-thinking skills and transfer them to your work.

   This game works best with four to eight participants in a group. We recommend that as many persons as possible get a chance to read aloud and act out parts in starred (*) vignettes. The game intends to make the examples vivid so you will recall the principles involved when you encounter similar situations.

2. Pick a moderator from the class to serve as referee, time keeper, and answer reader. (Your instructor may elect to be moderator.) Prior to the game, the moderator makes sure that both groups agree on some small reward(s) (actual or symbolic) to be awarded to the most successful group. Possible incentives include:
   a. Raisins—high scorers get ten raisins; low scorers get five.
   b. Help with a simple task—the low scorers give the high scorers ten minutes of help with a simple task they agree on. The high scorers give the low scorers five minutes of help with a task they agree on (e.g., help reviewing fallacy definitions).

   During the game, the moderator needs (1) a watch or timer that counts seconds, (2) access to the game's answer key in the Instructor's Manual, (3) a Reasoning-in-Practice (RIP) Ladder (see Exhibit 7.1), and (4) a pencil and paper to record and periodically announce group points on the Ladder as the game progresses. The moderator also will remind participants to hold their game cards so that others cannot see.

3. If the class contains twenty or fewer students, the moderator divides the class into halves, starting at any point, by counting off "one, two, three, four, five . . ." When all have counted off, the odds (Group A) go to one side of the room; the evens (Group B) go far enough away so that within-group discussions are not overheard by members of the other group. Where students number twenty or fewer, Groups A and B compete in a single game. If the class contains more than twenty students, the moderator divides

Exhibit 7.1

*Reasoning-in-Practice
(RIP) Ladder*

**Adjectives provided by
the Fall 1993 Methods
of Social Work Research
class at the University
of Wisconsin, Eau Claire.**

the class into an even number of groups (6 to 8 in a group) so that
Group A can compete against Group B; Group C can compete
against Group D, and so on. We find that more than one game
going on concurrently in the same room can get a little noisy.
If the noise gets too distracting where other rooms are available,
competing groups can conduct their games in other classrooms.

4. Each group picks a leader. Participants should sit in a circle facing each other, but far enough away from the other group so as not to be heard during private conversations.

5. When participants are ready, either read or act out the first vignette. Starred (*) items are acted out, unstarred items are read. Groups A and B take turns reading or acting out the vignettes. Ham it up if you like, but stick to the text.

6. After the vignette has been read or acted out, the moderator gives all participants at most *two minutes* to dial their game cards to the fallacy number that best describes the vignette. (You can make the Game Card from the last page of this Workbook.) Then participants place it face down so others cannot see it. Participants *do not discuss the item's content at this time,* but they can read the item to themselves and review the fallacy definitions.

7. As soon as all the members of a group have finished selecting a fallacy, they display their choice to others in their group.

8. After the two minutes are up, each leader tells the moderator whether their group is unanimous or has a disagreement. The moderator then consults Exhibit 7.2 to determine which group gets what points. The moderator gives points for unanimity only if the group's choice agrees with the answer key located in the Answers to Exercises section of the Instructors' Manual.

9. If both teams have some disagreement, each group talks privately to arrive at a choice. Each group's leader should try to assure that all members of his or her group get a chance to express an opinion. After a maximum of *three minutes* of discussion, the leader takes a vote, rotates his or her own choice card to make the majority choice, and places the card face down on the table, where it remains until the leader of the other group signals that his or her group has also made its choice. Then both leaders show the moderator their choice cards.

Exhibit 7.2

Awarding Points for the Reasoning-in-Practice Games

		GROUP A	
		All agree on the correct fallacy number.	Some do not agree on the fallacy number.
GROUP B	All agree on the correct fallacy number.	Group A gets 5 points. Group B gets 5 points.	Group A gets 0 points. Group B gets 5 points.
	Some do not agree on the fallacy number.	Group A gets 5 points. Group B gets 0 points.	Go to Step 9.

10. If both leaders mark the correct fallacy, both groups receive five points. If one group gets the correct answer, but the other doesn't, the former receives ten points. If both are wrong, then both receive no points, and the moderator writes the authors, telling us that we have written a vague vignette and definition.

11. This process continues until all the vignettes are finished, until the class runs out of time, or until one group gets 100 points and become Reasoners in Practice. The instructor may also decide that whoever has the most points at some predetermined time limit is the winner.

12. At the end of each game, both groups may be rewarded for participating, but the winning group should get the greater reward.

These procedures and rules are only suggested. If your group can agree on changes that make the game more fun, go for it! Please write to us describing changes that work for you and anything else that can help improve the game.

PLAYING THE GAME BY YOURSELF

You could work through each vignette and keep a score of your "hits" (correct fallacy spotting) and your "misses." The vignettes are laid out so they can be made into cards: copy the workbook pages onto card stock, then cut them apart. See where your total score places you on the Reasoning-in-Practice Ladder when you finish the game. You could also prepare a response to each item and compare your responses with suggestions provided by your instructor.

AN IMPORTANT TIP FOR AVOIDING CONFUSION

Play the game with just the fallacies listed for that game, because fallacies from different games can cause confusion (for example, Game C's Law of Small Numbers is very similar to Game A's Case Example).

Exercise 7

REASONING-IN-PRACTICE GAME A: COMMON PRACTICE FALLACIES

PURPOSE

To learn how to spot and avoid fallacies common to practice across the helping professions.

BACKGROUND

The nine common practice fallacies in this game stalk unwary practitioners in all helping professions. Watch for them creeping into thinking among participants in interdisciplinary case conferences when participants assume that a client's improvement following treatment was caused by the treatment (after this), that what may be true of a single individual or a handful should be true for all (case example), or that nonspecific descriptions of client outcomes constitute sufficient evidence to judge client improvement (vagueness).

INSTRUCTIONS

1. Please follow earlier Instructions for Games A, B, and C. Remember to act out starred (*) vignettes and read the others aloud (see Exhibit 7.11).
2. Read the description of each fallacy.

DEFINITIONS, EXAMPLES, AND COUNTERMEASURES

1. *Relying on Case Examples:* **drawing conclusions about many clients from only one or a few unrepresentative individuals.** A generalization is made about the effectiveness of a method, or about what is typically true of clients based on one or just a few clients. We can easily become immersed in the details of a case, forgetting that it is just one instance. Stanovich (1992, p. 55) describes a case example as "virtually worthless" as evidence. Case examples often portray individuals so vividly that their emotional appeal detracts from seeking evidence about what helps clients or is generally true of clients. Case examples also encourage oversimplification of what may be very complex problems. They are notoriously open to intentional and unintentional bias, including behavioral confirmation effects (seeking examples that support favored assumptions and overlooking

contradictory evidence). If one searches long enough for it, a case can be found that will support almost any conclusion (see Exhibit 7.3). This is not to say that case material cannot be valuable. For example, case material can be used to demonstrate practice skills. A videotape of an interview with an adolescent mother may demonstrate practice competencies. A field instructor may model a family therapy technique. Such use of case material is a valuable part of professional education. The problem arises only if you generalize to all clients from case examples.

Example: A two-year-old boy with behavior problems who had been placed in a regular foster home was about to be removed and placed elsewhere because the family, with whom the child had a strong attachment, could not manage his behavior. Arranging day

Exhibit 7.3

"And now I would like you to meet our typical resident."

treatment allowed the boy to stay in his foster home. Day treatment made it much easier for the foster family to provide a good environment for the child and to deal with visits from the biological mother, to whom the boy will probably return (Stepleton, 1989, pp. 268). Because of this case, I believe that day treatment effectively helps troubled foster children.

Countermeasures. To make accurate generalizations about a population, collect a representative sample from this population. You may use observation and surveys. To judge whether or not client change is related to a particular intervention, search for experimental studies using randomized assignment of clients to different groups. Such studies are published in the professional literature.

2. *Relying on Testimonials:* **claims that a method is effective based on one's own experience.** Testimonials are often given in professional conferences, in professional publications, or on film or videotape. Clients may report how much participating in a particular treatment benefitted them. To qualify as a testimonial, a person must (1) assert that a given method was helpful, (2) offer his or her own experience as evidence that the method works, and (3) describe the experience, not to demonstrate how the treatment method is applied, but to prove that the method is effective. Testimonials do not provide evidence that a treatment is effective. Though people who give testimonials are generally sincere (Cramp & Simmons, 1936), their sincerity does not assure their accuracy. Those who give a testimonial may feel pressure to please the person who requested their testimonial. Promoters often choose people to give testimonials because of their personal attractiveness, charismatic qualities, and other features that may play on an audience's emotions. Those who give testimonials may not have been trained to make the systematic and objective observations they would need to determine if change truly has occurred (see Exhibit 7.4).

Example: "After taking so many other medicines without being helped, you can imagine how happy and surprised I felt when I discovered that Natex was doing me a lot of good. Natex seemed to go right to the root of my trouble, helped my appetite and put an end to the indigestion, gas and shortness of breath." (Local lady took Natex year ago—had good health ever since, 1935, May 27, p. 7). This woman's testimonial appeared on the same page of a newspaper as her obituary.

Countermeasures: Conduct a controlled study to evaluate the effects of the treatment or consult literature that describes such studies. Both case examples and testimonials involve partiality in the use of evidence—looking at just part of the picture. They rely on selected instances, which often give a biased view.

3. *Vagueness:* **vague descriptions of problems, related outcomes and progress measures, which may make it impossible to determine if any progress has been made. A problem may be**

Exhibit 7.4

stated imprecisely. For example, specific problem-related behaviors, thoughts, or feelings may not be noted. Vague progress measures make it impossible to know whether specific outcomes have been accomplished. Vague terms foster fuzzy thinking (Thouless, 1974), and they obscure the results of efforts to help individuals, groups, and communities. Examples of vague terms that describe outcomes include *improved, better, coming along nicely, somewhat better, functioning at a higher level,* and *substantially improved.* If the client "improved" without our defining how, how would we know if this were the case? Examples of clear outcomes include initiating three conversations a day (a conversation is defined as more than a greeting and at least one minute long), or spending half an hour playing with your child each weekday after school, or signing up three neighbors in the next week to babysit for Mrs. X an hour each week in the evening.

Example: "Our community organization efforts have been effective. I noted after six weeks of town meetings that the residents of Burnside seem to feel more in charge."

Countermeasures: Clearly describe problems, related outcomes, and progress measures. Descriptions of outcomes should be so clearly stated that people can agree on when they have been attained. The descriptions should answer the questions What? Where? When? Who? and How often?

4. *Assuming Softhearted Therefore Softheaded:* **the mistaken belief that one cannot be both a warm, empathic, caring person and an analytical, scientific, rational thinker.** There are two important dimensions to the helping process:

(1) a caring, empathic attitude; (2) skill in offering effective methods. As Meehl (1973) argued, it is precisely because clinicians do care (are softhearted) that they should rely on the best evidence available (be hardheaded) when making judgments. Softheartedness is a necessary, but not a sufficient condition in the helping process. Assuming that one has to be either caring or rational misses the point: A person can be both.

Paul Meehl (1973) first exposed the fallacy that he called "Identifying the Softhearted with the Softheaded." He documented in 1954 that, in spite of the fact that statistical prediction (statistical tables based on experience with many clients)

Exhibit 7.5

Four Practitioner Types

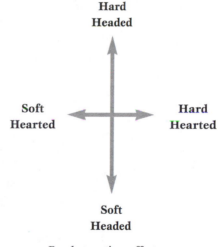

Type I

Soft Hearted/
Hard Headed

(Ideal)

Concerned about effects of methods, persists when asking questions, asks specific questions, devises tests to measure effectiveness, bases conclusions on facts properly evaluated, tries to answer questions objectively, identifies key elements in arguments before reacting to them, not easily led in sheeplike fashion, believes in tests to verify ideas.

Type II

Hard Hearted/
Hard Headed

Able to reflect feelings of others accurately, a good listener, more comfortable dealing with people than with things, senses when others need help, concerned about social injustice, resolves to help others, likely to put concerns of others ahead of own, finds others come to talk about problems.

Hard Headed

Soft Hearted — **Hard Hearted**

Soft Headed

Uses the pronoun *I* excessively, more comfortable dealing with things than with people, believes that those in trouble must get themselves out, puts own concerns ahead of others, unconcerned about social justice, jumps in to tell of own problems when others talk of their problems, lacks empathy.

Type III

Soft Hearted/
Soft Headed

(Dangerous Combination)

Rarely questions effects of methods, easily discouraged or distracted when approaching a problem, gullible and swayed by emotional appeals, asks vague questions, thinks "one opinion is as good as another," reacts to arguments without identifying elements in the arguments, jumps to conclusions, follows the crowd, believes in magic.

Type IV

Hard Hearted/
Soft Headed

Source: L. E. Gibbs, *Scientific Reasoning for Social Workers,* p. 36. Copyright 1991 by Merrill, an imprint of Macmillan Publishing Company. Reprinted by permission.

consistently outpredicted judgments made by senior clinicians, helpers still relied on their gut-level feelings when making important predictions. Statistical procedures have been used to predict suicide (Motto, Heilbron, & Juster, 1985), the likelihood of a new criminal offense (Hoffman, 1986), and adjustment in a foster home (Stone & Stone, 1983). Over 100 studies now support Meehl's conclusions about the superiority of statistical prediction over gut-level feelings (Dawes, Faust, & Meehl, 1989). Meehl (1973) speculated that clinicians often ignore better statistical evidence because they believe that they would be less feeling and caring about clients if they based their judgments on statistical evidence (see Exhibit 7.6).

Example:

"Today it seems more apparent that the research stance and the posture of the therapist are quite the opposite of each other. The researcher must keep distant from his data, be objective, and not intrude on or influence what he is studying. He must also explore and explain all the complex variables of every issue, since he is a seeker after truth [why wouldn't a therapist want to know the truth too?]. The therapist's stance is quite different. He must be personally involved and human, not distant and objective" (Haley, 1980, p. 17).

Countermeasures: Be hardheaded (analytical, scientific, data-driven) because you are softhearted (really do care about what helps people).

Exhibit 7.6

5. *Being Biased/Not Objective:* **being so committed to support a particular view that evidence and arguments that run counter to that view are ignored or not reported.** This is a *motivational* source of fallacy. It is a one-sided way of thinking that results in poor decisions because helpful data and new ideas are overlooked.

   Example: "In matters controversial, my perception's rather fine. I always see both points of view: the one that's wrong and mine." For other examples of biased/not objective thinking, see professional advertisements, presentations at professional conferences by those seeking to sell their method of intervention (particularly if they want you to pay for their training), and literature reviews by instructors who present only one point of view about an issue.

   Countermeasures: Be skeptical of anyone who presents just one side of anything. The world's not that simple. Seek and present alternative views and data in your own work. How else can you arrive at approximations to the truth? The more you are committed to a particular view, the more vigorously you should seek counterevidence.

6. *Relying on Newness/Tradition:* **a fallacy if: (1) an assertion is made about how to help clients, or what is true of clients; (2) the assertion is said to be true because it has been held to be true or practiced for a long time (tradition), or because the idea or practice has just been developed (newness), and (3) no studies or data are given to support the claim.** The practice of bleeding (applying leeches, cutting into a vein with a scalpel) as a treatment for infection was practiced for hundreds of years (Haller, 1981), in spite of the fact that there was no evidence that it worked (see Exhibit 7.7). Conversely, the mere fact that a treatment method has just been developed does not insure its effectiveness. All treatments were new at some time, including ones that promised great effectiveness but were later found to be ineffective or even harmful. For example, the sex hormone DES was enthusiastically adopted in the 1940s and early 1950s to treat various problems with pregnancy even though there had been no careful evaluation using randomized control trials. Tragically, DES was found to produce cancer in the daughters of women who had been treated with DES (Apfel & Fisher, 1984; Berendes & Lee, 1993).

   Example of Appeal to Tradition: A nursing home social worker says, "We have always classified our residents according to their level of nursing care on the four floors of Rest Haven. No matter what reasons you might give for changing this practice, I doubt that the administration would change a practice that has been in place for many years."

   Example of Appeal to Newness: "This method of family therapy is described in a new book by Dr. Gerbels. It's the latest method. We should use it here."

Countermeasures: Point out that being new or old does not make an idea or practice valid. Ask to see evidence and data to judge the effects of methods.

7. ***Accepting Uncritical Documentation (Gullibility):*** **the mistaken belief that if an idea has been described in the literature (book, journal article, newspaper), it must be true. To be classified as uncritical documentation, literature must be cited, but no information at all given about the method by**

Exhibit 7.7

Death of General
George Washington

The death of this illustrious man, by an abrupt and violent distemper, will long occupy the attention of his fellow citizens. No public event could have occurred, adapted so strongly to awaken the sensibility and excite the reflections of Americans. No apology will therefore be needful for relating the circumstances of this great event. The particulars of his disease and death being stated by the physicians who attended him, their narrative deserves to be considered as authentic. The following account was drawn up by Doctors Craik and Dick.

"Some time in the night of Friday, the 13th of December, having been exposed to a rain on the preceding day, General Washington was attacked with an inflammatory affection of the upper part of the wind pipe, called, in technical language, *Cynanche Trachealis*. The disease commenced with a violent ague, accompanied with some pain in the upper and fore part of the throat, a sense of stricture in the same part, a cough, and a difficult, rather than a painful, deglutition, which were soon succeeded by fever and a quick and laborious respiration. The necessity of blood-letting suggesting itself to the General, he procured a bleeder in the neighbourhood, who took from his arm, in the night, twelve or fourteen ounces of blood. He could not be prevailed on by the family, to send for the attending physician till the following morning, who arrived at Mount Vernon at about eleven o'clock on Saturday. Discovering the case to be highly alarming, and foreseeing the fatal tendency of the disease, two consulting physicians were immediately sent for, who arrived, one at half after three, and the other at four o'clock in the afternoon: in the mean time were employed two copious bleedings, a blister was applied to the part affected, two moderate doses of calomel were given, and an injection was administered, which operated on the lower intestines, but all without any perceptible advantage, the respiration becoming still more difficult and painful. On the arrival of the first of the consulting physicians, it was agreed, as there were yet no signs of accumulation in the bronchial vessels of the lungs, to try the effect of another bleeding, when about thirty-two ounces of blood were drawn, without the least apparent alleviation of the disease. Vapours of vinegar and water were frequently inhaled, ten grains of calomel were given, succeeded by repeated doses of emetic tartar, amounting in all to five or six grains, with no other effect than a copious discharge from the bowels. The power of life seemed now manifestly yielding to the force of the disorder; blisters were applied to the extremities, together with a cataplasm of bran and vinegar to the throat. Speaking, which had been painful from the beginning, now became almost impracticable: respiration grew more and more contracted and imperfect, till half after eleven on Saturday night, when, retaining the full possession of his intellects, he expired without a struggle!

Source: Death of General George Washington. (1799). *The Monthly Magazine and American Review*, 1(6), 475–477.

which the cited author arrived at a particular conclusion (no studies, measures, observations by competent observers, or discussion of how the conclusion was drawn). Even the most preposterous ideas have advocates. For example, see the *National Enquirer* to find that Elvis still lives and that a woman revived her gerbil after it had been frozen stiff in her freezer for six months.

Example: According to Zingg (1941), whose article appeared in *Scientific American,*

> In 1929, when I first heard of wolf-children, my reaction, no doubt like that of everyone else, was that such stories were stuff and nonsense. However, when the study of other scientific problems brought me back to the subject of wolf-children, I found evidence of some respectability for about 30 cases of feral or wild man.... The best of these cases is that of the wolf-children of Midnapore, India.... The two wolf-children of India were first seen living as wolves among wolves.... (p. 135)

Countermeasures: If you want to know whether to believe an assertion that is merely referenced, you'll need to read that reference for yourself.

8. *After This—Post Hoc Ergo Propter Hoc (after this therefore because of this):* **the mistaken belief that if event A precedes event B in time, then event A has caused B** (Chaffee, 1988; Engel, 1994). Practitioners often use temporal order as a causal cue (Einhorn & Hogarth, 1986). As Medawar notes, "If a person (a) feels poorly or is sick, (b) receives treatment to make him better, and (c) gets better, then no power of reasoning known to medical science can convince him that it may not have been the treatment that restored his health" (1967, pp. 14–15). If A causes B, it is true that A must precede B, but there may be many other events preceding B that could be the cause. A's preceding B is a *necessary* but not a *sufficient* (always enough) condition to infer cause. Let's consider an example: Robins migrate north to Wisconsin each year. Shortly after the robins arrive, the flowers start to bloom; therefore, robins cause flowers to bloom.

This fallacy occurs in practice when (1) a problem exists, (2) the practitioner takes action to remove the complaint (event A), and (3) the complaint disappears (event B). The practitioner then assumes that his or her action caused the complaint to disappear. The practitioner takes credit for effective action when, in fact, some other event may have caused the change.

Example: "Mr. James just started our support group for the recently bereaved and a few meetings later seemed to be much less depressed. That support group must work."

Countermeasures: Think of other possible causes for client improvement, or deterioration, before taking responsibility for it. For example, you may think that your client acquired a new social skill as a result of your program, but your client may have learned it from interactions with friends or family. You may believe that cognitive behavioral therapy helped a depressed middle-aged male client, but the client may have improved because he saw a psychiatrist who prescribed an antidepressant. A break in hot weather, rather than your community crisis team's efforts to head off violence, may have been responsible for a decrease in street violence. There are cyclical problems that get worse, improve, and again get worse. A large percentage of medical problems clear up by themselves (Skrabanek & McCormick, 1992). A well-designed study can help rule out these and other explanations of client change.

9. *Focusing Only on Successes:* **inferring that a method is effective by recalling only individual cases where improvement followed use of the method. Failure, instances of spontaneous recovery, and persons not treated who got worse are ignored.** When people examine an association to infer cause, they often rely on evidence that confirms their hypothesis, that is, those who were in treatment and improved; see Cell A in Exhibit 7.8 (Schustack & Sternberg, 1981). Those who consider evidence like that shown in Exhibit 7.8 tend to pay attention Cell A (got treatment and improved), then Cell B, then Cell C, and finally Cell D in this order (p. 111).

    Example: "Dr. Rudie had ten cases of depression that responded to Prozac. I think it is probably effective."

    Countermeasures: All four cells must be examined to get an accurate picture of whether an intervention works. In addition to considering successes, look for failures, persons not treated who got better, and those not treated who got worse. Decrease reliance on memory (Arkes, 1981). Keep records of successes, failures, those not treated and improved, and those not treated and not improved. The latter two groups might be estimated by reading literature about what generally happens to untreated persons. Look fearlessly at all the evidence, not just the data that support a hypothesis (i.e., cases where the treatment worked). How else can an accurate judgment be made?

10. *Nonfallacy Items:* **items that do not contain fallacies.** In these items, a fallacy is named and avoided (e.g., "You are attacking me personally, not examining my argument; that's an ad hominem appeal"), or the helper applies sound reasoning and evidence (e.g., cites and critiques a study, uses a valid outcome measure to judge client change).

    Use Exhibit 7.9 to review the names of the fallacies.

Exhibit 7.8

Examining the Association Between Treatment and Outcome

Client Outcome

		Improved	Not Improved	
Client Participated in Treatment	Yes	Cell A Successes $N = 75$	Cell B Failures $N = 35$	Proportion Successful $= \dfrac{A}{A + B} \times 100$
	No	Cell C Spontaneous Recovery $N = 40$	Cell D Untreated, Unimproved $N = 60$	Proportion in Spontaneous Recovery $= \dfrac{C}{C + D} \times 100$

Source: L. E. Gibbs, *Scientific Reasoning for Social Workers,* p. 70. Copyright 1991 by Merrill, an imprint of Macmillan Publishing Company. Reprinted by permission.

Exhibit 7.9

Fallacies in Game A

No.	Name
1.	Case Examples
2.	Testimonials
3.	Vagueness (vague descriptions of problems, outcomes, and/or progress measures)
4.	Assuming Softhearted, Therefore, Softheaded
5.	Being Biased/Not Objective
6.	Reliance on Newness/Tradition
7.	Accepting Uncritical Documentation (Gullibility)
8.	After This—Post Hoc Ergo Propter Hoc
9.	Focusing Only on Successes
10.	Nonfallacy Item

Exhibit 7.10   **VIGNETTES FOR GAME A:
COMMON PRACTICE FALLACIES**

Your Name   Date

Course

Instructor's Name

REMINDERS

Act out the starred (*) items (3, 9, 13). Take turns reading the others out loud. Remember that some items do not contain fallacies. In these items, a fallacy is named and avoided (e.g., "You are attacking me personally, not examining my argument; that's an ad hominem appeal"), or the helper applies sound reasoning and evidence (e.g., cites and critiques a study, applies a valid outcome measure to judge change). Use Exhibit 7.9 to review the names of the fallacies.

1. *Client speaking to potential clients:* I participated in six weekly encounter-group meetings conducted by Sally Rogers, my social worker, and the group helped. My scores on the Coopersmith Self-Esteem Inventory have increased. I recommend that you attend the group too.

2. *One social worker speaking to another:* I think that Tom's chemical dependency problem and codependency have definitely worsened in the past six months.

*3. *Two administrators speaking with each other:*
    First administrator: In what proportion of hard-to-place adoption cases did the child remain in the placement home at least two years?
    Second administrator: We have had fifty successful placements in the past two years.
    First administrator: How many did we try to place? I'm trying to get some idea of our success rate.
    Second administrator: We don't have information about that.

4. *Politician critical of welfare benefits and welfare fraud among recipients of Aid for Dependent Children:* One "welfare queen" illustrates the extent of the problem. She used twelve fictitious names, forged several birth certificates, claimed fifty nonexistent children as dependents, received Aid for Families with Dependent Children (AFDC) for ten years, and defrauded the state of Michigan out of $400,000. She drove an expensive car, took vacations in Mexico, and lived in an expensive house.

5. *Psychologist:* Our agency offers communication enrichment workshops for couples having some rough spots in their relationships. Four to five couples participated as a group in ten weekly two-hour sessions. Each participant completed the Inventory of Family Feelings (IFF) during the first and last meetings. These scores show marked improvement. Our workshops enhance positive feelings.

6. *A supervisor arguing against critical thinking:* There are two kinds of helpers: those who have people skills and who can interact warmly with clients, and those who lack this natural gift but try to make up for it by consulting studies, measures, surveys, and other such trash.

7. *Author in a professional journal:* This literature review summarizes six articles. Our library assistants were instructed to find articles that support the effectiveness of family-based treatment. All six articles support the effectiveness of family-based treatment for adolescent runaways and related problems.

8. *Psychiatrist:* My client, Mr. Harrison, had a Beck Depression Inventory (BDI) score that placed him in the severe range when I saw him at intake. I worked with him using cognitive behavioral methods for six weeks. In the seventh week, his score was in the normal range. My methods worked with Mr. Harrison. His BDI scores were higher after treatment.

*9. *A student speaking to her advisor:*
   Student: My study included forty subjects, and I was able to contact thirty on the follow-up.
   Advisor: Ahum. That's OK.
   Student: When I analyzed data from these thirty, I found a statistically significant difference favoring our treatment. Then data came in from five more cases. When I added these to the analysis, the results were no longer statistically significant. What should I do now?
   Advisor: You had such neat results before the new data came in. The results still run in the expected direction. So, let's just omit the data from the new cases. After all, if the data had come in a little later, you wouldn't have even had the opportunity to analyze them.

10. *Participant in a program for nicotine addicts:* The Smokeless Program conducted by the social worker at Mercy Hospital helped me to stop smoking—I tried unsuccessfully for ten years! Every morning I barked like a trained seal, my cough was so bad. I liked especially the way the program made me aware of how much I was smoking by putting every cigarette on a chart that we attached to our cigarette pack. That showed me when and how much I smoked each day. Just seeing my record brought me up short. I stopped smoking completely by the third meeting, and I have not smoked in ten weeks. You should try this program.

11. *Teacher questioning whether a suicide-prevention program should be initiated:* Shaffer and others (1990) studied the effectiveness of a 1.5- to 3-hour suicide-prevention program on 1,551 ninth- and tenth-grade students. Among sixty-three who said they had attempted suicide (thirty-five attempters who attended the program and twenty-eight attempters who served in a comparison group), the statistical analysis that compared program attenders ($n = 35$) against the comparison group ($n = 28$) showed no significant difference in a measure of attitudes across the groups. "Program exposure did not significantly influence previous attempters' deviant attitudes" (p. 3,154). I recognize that this is only one study, but it is the best that I was able to find. Based on this study, I doubt whether this kind of suicide-prevention program affects suicide-related attitudes.

12. *Senior practitioner speaking to a field-work student:* If you try to measure your client's progress, you will destroy your rapport with the client. Clients know when they are being treated like a guinea pig and resent it. You will be better off if you rely on your intuition and attend to how you react toward your client. As I see it, you're either an intuitive type or an automaton.

*13. *Dean of School of Arts and Sciences speaking to the Chair of the Department of Social Work:*

   Dean: How did the social-work majors who graduated last June fare in the job market during their first six months after graduation?

   Department Chair: We've been pretty successful. Thirty are employed in social work, and one is in graduate school.

14. *Speech therapist speaking to a teacher:* Have you heard about facilitated communication? It has just been developed as a way to communicate with autistic children. A facilitator can help the child type messages out on a computer keyboard that communicates the child's thoughts. These thoughts would remain locked in the child without this new technology and its skillful use.

15. *An advertisement, including pictures of Bill in* The American Journal of Psychiatry: **Name:** Bill. **Occupation:** Unemployed administrative assistant. **Age:** 48. **Height:** 5′10.″ **Weight:** 170 lb. **History:** Patient complains of fatigue, inability to concentrate, and feelings of worthlessness since staff cuts at the corporation where he worked for 21 years resulted in the loss of his job. He has failed to begin a company-sponsored program and to look for a new job. **Initial Treatment:** After 2 months of antidepressant treatment, patient complained of sexual dysfunction (erectile failure and decreased libido), which had not been a problem prior to antidepressant treatment. . . . **Recommendation:** Discontinue current antidepressant and switch to a new-generation, non-serotonergic antidepressant. Start Wellbutrin to relieve depression and minimize risk of sexual dysfunction. **Outcome After 4 Weeks of Therapy With Wellbutrin:** Patient reports feeling more energetic. Sexual performance is normal. He has enrolled in job retraining program. . . . **Wellbutrin (BUPROPION HCL) relieves depression with few life-style disruptions.** (WELLBUTRIN, 1992, A33–35)

16. *An administrator in a group home for developmentally disabled adults:* According to Bird, Dores, Moniz, and Robinson (1989), functional-communication training reduced severe aggressive and self-injurious behaviors in self-injuring adults. Let's try this method with Mark and Olie.

17. *Director of a refuge home for battered women:* The women who attend our program for physically and emotionally abused women report on their levels of self-esteem. Generally, their self-esteem improves.

18. *One physician to another:* Clancy, Cebul, and Williams (1988) provide the best evidence available about whether knowledge of clinical decision analysis transfers to decision making in everyday practice.

19. *Child-welfare worker to students in class:* Open adoption is one of the newest advances in adoptions. In open adoption, the biological parents are allowed to stay in touch with the adoptive parents, and in many cases, the biological parents contribute to rearing the child. Your agency should try this increasingly popular option.

20. *Client treated by a chiropractor:* Mrs. Sisneros was experiencing lower-back pain. She saw her chiropractor, felt better afterward, and concluded that the chiropractor helped her back.

FOLLOW-UP QUESTION

Do any of this game's vignettes reflect real situations particularly well? Which one(s)?

_____

_____

_____

_____

_____

_____

_____

Exercise 8
REASONING-IN-PRACTICE GAME B: GROUP AND INTERPERSONAL DYNAMICS

PURPOSE

To learn how to identify and avoid fallacies that often occur in case conferences, staffings, interdisciplinary teams, conferences, etc.

BACKGROUND

Groupwork is a common part of practice including, for example, group cognitive therapy with depressed older persons, and task-centered work with the mentally ill. Everyday practice requires participation in a variety of groups (e.g., multidisciplinary teams, case conferences, task groups, seminars, workshops, and hospital rounds) where decisions are made that affect the lives of clients. Many groups involve both professionals and laypersons such as self-help groups and support groups. Community-action groups include neighborhood block organizations, conflict-resolution groups, miners' family advocacy groups, and other grass-roots organizations.

Groups provide many advantages, including multiple points of view, different approaches to problems, diverse experiences, and a variety of skills and knowledge among members. On the other hand, without sound leadership and knowledge and skills regarding group process and practice fallacies, groups may make unwise decisions. The nine practice fallacies described can occur without your awareness and stall, sidetrack, or stop effective group process.

INSTRUCTIONS

1. Before playing Game B, review the instructions located before Exercise 7.
2. Read the descriptions of each fallacy given in Exercise 8 including the definition, example, and suggested counter-measures. This will help you become familiar with the game, the fallacies addressed in Exercise 8, and how to avoid them.
3. Read each vignette aloud when playing the game. This will make the situations more real. Starred (*) items require volunteers to take turns acting out the example while others follow along in the script or watch the actors (see Exhibit 8.2).

1. *Ad Hominem (At the Person):* **attacking (or praising) the person, or feeling attacked (or praised) as a person, rather than examining the substance of an argument.** Arguing ad hominem is the reverse of arguing ad rem (at the thing). The ad hominem fallacy may arise when someone lacks supporting evidence but nonetheless wants his or her point of view to prevail. Instead of addressing the substance of another person's argument, he or she may seek to discredit the person by calling the person a name or by attacking the person's character or motives (Chase, 1956).

    Example: Joel Fischer (1973) published a review of studies about the effectiveness of social casework. He concluded that casework was ineffective and might even be harmful. One opponent accused Fischer of being "in a bag" (Crumb, 1973, p. 124).

    Countermeasures: Address the issue. Argue ad rem. Confine your attention to defining problems clearly and examining the evidence related to claims. A standard for evaluating evidence can be found in the Quality of Study Rating Form (Exercise 12).

2. **Appeal to Authority (Ad Verecundium): an attempt to buffalo an opponent into accepting a conclusion by playing on the opponent's reluctance to question the conclusion of someone who has a high status or who is viewed as the expert** (Engel, 1994, pp. 208–210).

    Example: A master of ceremonies introduces a speaker to a professional audience: "Dr. MacMillan is one of the most renowned neurolinguistic programmers in the world. He has published three books on neurolinguistic programming therapy, and he now holds the prestigious William B. Day Lectureship at the University of Pennsylvania. His reputation supports what he'll tell us about the effectiveness of his approach.

    Countermeasures: Ask to see the authority's evidence and evaluate that.

3. *Diversion (Red Herring):* **an attempt to sidetrack people from one argument to another so as never to deal effectively with the first** (Capaldi, 1979, pp. 128–129). *Red herring* originally referred to a fugitive's use of dead fish scent to throw tracking dogs off the trail. Sometimes unethical adversaries create a diversion because they know their argument is too weak to stand up to careful scrutiny; they sidetrack the group's attention to a different topic (they drag a red herring across the trail of the discussion). More commonly, the diversion just happens as attention wanders, gets piqued by a new interest, or is side-tracked by humor.

    Example: Discussion during a case conference:

    Paul: Edna, my eighty-seven-year-old client, lives alone. She has looked frail lately, and I'm worried that she is not eating a balanced diet. Her health seems generally good, no major weaknesses or injuries, just dietary problems. What do you think of her as a candidate for the Meals-on-Wheels Program?

Craig: I saw a Meals-on-Wheels meal recently. Ooftah! The fish looked pulpy.

John: Speaking of fish, did you know that the Walleyed Pike were biting last Sunday on Halfmoon Lake?

Countermeasures: Gently bring the discussion back to the point at issue (e.g., We were just talking about . . .).

4. *Stereotyping:* **"A stereotype is an oversimplified generalization about a class of individuals, one based on a presumption that every member of the class has some set of properties that is (probably erroneously) identified with the class"** (Moore & Parker, 1986, p. 160). "The stereotype strips a person of his complexity and his individuality and reduces him to one quality" (Gula, 1979, p. 40). Research shows that stereotypes based on sex (Kurtz, Johnson, & Rice, 1989), race (Cousins, Fischer, Glisson, & Kameoka, 1986) and attractiveness (Johnson, Kurtz, Tomlinson, & Howe, 1986; Nordholm, 1980) influence practice decisions. Stereotypes can bias judgments, including notions about what to expect from persons from low socioeconomic backgrounds. Stereotyping about clients is a particularly pernicious fallacy in practice because it can lead to erroneous judgments and decisions about how to help individual clients.

   Example:

   Income maintenance worker: I think that Mrs. Owens is probably a typical low-income client. She lacks the coping skills she needs to be an effective parent.

   Countermeasures: Judge individuals and their ideas from a careful assessment of their behavior and thinking, not from some preconceived notion about what to expect from them because of their membership in some group or class of individuals. Racism, sexism, classism, and ageism are based on stereotypes that can lead to inappropriately negative or positive attitudes and behaviors toward individuals.

5. *Manner or Style:* **believing an argument because of the apparent sincerity, speaking voice, attractiveness, stage presence, likability, or other stylistic traits of an argument's presenter.** The reverse of this argument, not believing an argument because you find the speaker's style or appearance offensive or distracting, can also be a problem. This fallacy captures many gullible victims in this age of television, videotape, film, and videodisc. Beware of advertisements for treatment facilities, as well as slick descriptions and portrayals of intervention methods that focus on how pleasant and clean the facilities' grounds are or how enthusiastically attractive clients may advocate the program. Slick propagandistic portrayals are often used in place of data about attained outcomes (e.g., What percentage of clients benefit in what ways? How do we know? Do any clients get worse?).

Example:

First student: Take Ames's class. You'll love it. She has a quick sense of humor that will leave you laughing. She rivals some stand-up comics that I have seen on TV for her sense of humor.

Second student: I was wondering what I'd learn in Ames's class.

First student: Forget that. You'll see what I mean.

Countermeasures: Base your judgments and decisions on the evidence presented, not on the speaker's style or lack of it. Even if the idea comes from an "odd duck," only the idea's utility and soundness matter.

6. *Groupthink:* **the tendency for group members (e.g., of interdisciplinary teams, task groups, service-coordination groups, staff) to avoid sharing useful opinions or data with the group because they fear they might be "put down," hurt the feelings of other group members, or cause disunity.** Janis (1971, November) gives this definition of groupthink: "I use the term Groupthink as a quick and easy way to refer to the mode of thinking that persons engage in when concurrence-seeking [seeking agreement] becomes so dominant in a cohesive group that it tends to override realistic appraisal of alternative courses of action" (p. 43). Groupthink undermines a group's critical thinking by preventing or stopping the discussion of important ideas that might have guided the group to a sound decision. Unless a culture of inquiry is encouraged, groups may stifle dissenting opinion. Indicators of groupthink include stereotyping or characterizing the leaders of opposing groups as evil or incompetent, exerting direct pressure on group members to stay in line, or fostering an [incorrect] belief that group members are unanimous in their opinion (Janis, 1971, November).

Example: A student in her tenth week of an introduction to social work enjoys class. She admires and respects the instructor and several members of the class. She hears the instructor say something about an important point that she knows is wrong, but she decides not bring it up because she thinks doing so would "cause a stink."

Countermeasures: Janis (1982) suggests three ways to counter groupthink: (1) assign the role of critical evaluator to some of the group's members, (2) indicate at the beginning of a discussion that the leader will be impartial to the group's decision, and (3) for important decisions, set up independent policy-planning committees to gather evidence and deliberate independently of the other groups, with each planning committee led by a different person (pp. 262–265).

7. *Bandwagon:* **"Wherever there is an attempt to persuade us that a claim is true or an action right because it is popular— because many, most, or all people believe it or do it, because the crowd is going in that direction—we have . . . the bandwagon appeal"** (Freeman, 1993, p. 56). Examples involve the belief that, if many people accept a particular conclusion

about clients or many people use a particular treatment method, then the conclusion must be true or the treatment must be effective. The bandwagon appeal implies that by the sheer weight of numbers of people, the point in question cannot be wrong.

Example: Two social workers speaking over lunch in a cafeteria of an alcohol and other drug abuse (AODA) treatment facility:

First social worker: A lot of the AODA treatment facilities in our area seem to be adopting the matching hypothesis. More and more facilities try to systematically match clients with treatment.

Second social worker: I agree. I think we should too.

Countermeasures: Critically evaluate popular notions, particularly those concerning treatment. Look at studies, client data, counterevidence, and counterarguments before you join the herd.

8. ***Either-Or (False Dilemma):*** **stating or implying that there are only two alternatives open to the group, which denies the chance to think of other options.** Either-or reasoning prematurely limits options for problem solving. "An argument that presumes that there are only two ways of looking at a situation—or that only one of two choices can be made—when actually other alternatives do exist, is guilty of the either-or fallacy, or false dilemma" (Mayfield, 1991, p. 312).

Example: "The way I see it, you're either for us, or you're against us. Which is it?"

Countermeasures: Identify alternative views of what might be done. Ask each group member to write down independently a list of possible courses of action. Assure group members that whatever they write will be read anonymously and discussed seriously.

9. ***Straw Man Argument:*** **misrepresenting a person's argument and then attacking the misrepresentation.** "If you criticize a position that an author did not really hold, and infer from your criticism that his real position is flawed, you have committed the straw man fallacy" (Govier, 1985, p. 104).

Example:

Alicia: The University Hospital's Human Subjects Committee should be informed about this ethical violation. A patient came in with extremely low blood sugar, but the experiment's protocol called for a delay in administering sugar; so, the patient's brain is damaged now, possibly because of the delay. I think someone ought to investigate this incident, and the patient may deserve compensation.

Billy Joe: Your argument that the *committee* behaved unethically simply does not hold water. The members of that committee are beyond reproach. They are so conservative in their guidelines that no experiment that they have approved would be designed in a way that would violate patient rights.

Countermeasures: Accurately represent other positions. Carefully listen to another person's position; restate that position in your own words as accurately as you can; listen to hear whether you have restated the position accurately—then react.

10. *Nonfallacy Items:* **items that do not include a fallacy.** Be ready for a few examples of sound reasoning.

Use the list in Exhibit 8.1 as reminders of fallacies reviewed in this exercise.

	No.	Name
Exhibit 8.1	1.	Ad Hominem (At the Person)
	2.	Appeal to Authority (Ad Verecundium)
Fallacies in Game B	3.	Diversion (Red Herring)
	4.	Stereotyping
	5.	Manner or Style
	6.	Groupthink
	7.	Bandwagon
	8.	Either-Or (False Dilemma)
	9.	Straw Man Argument
	10.	Nonfallacy Item

Exhibit 8.2   **VIGNETTES FOR GAME B:**
GROUP AND INTERPERSONAL DYNAMICS

Your Name   Date
_____

Course
_____

Instructor's Name
_____

REMINDER

The vignettes are more vivid if each item is read aloud. The starred (*)
items may be more effective and fun if class members act out the parts.
Refer to Exhibit 8.1 for a summary of fallacies.

---

*1. *Situation:* A multidisciplinary team (special education teacher,
     school psychologist, speech therapist, social worker, and child's
     parent) have just finished a meeting to decide if Jason, age four,
     should be admitted to an Early Childhood-Exceptional Educa-
     tion Needs (EC-EEN) program.

     Special-education teacher: I know that Jason's score on the
     Battelle Developmental Inventory was above the cutoff score
     for admission to our program, but I think that Jason's behavior,
     as I saw it during his visit to my classroom, qualifies him for
     admission to the EC-EEN program. He ran around the room
     almost all the time, was not task-focused, and did not follow
     instructions.

     School psychologist: Maybe you're right. Why didn't you say
     something about this during the team meeting?

     Special-education teacher: Nobody, including the parents,
     seemed to think that Jason's behavior was a problem except me.

     School psychologist: It's really too bad that you didn't feel com-
     fortable enough to bring this up. You were the team member
     who had the best chance to observe him.

---

*2. *Situation:* Case conference at a home for the mentally ill:

First social worker: The aide who works daily with Mr. Dewitt, a twenty-four-year-old schizophrenic, told me that yesterday Mr. Dewitt showed an increasing potential for violence. He said that Mr. Dewitt seems to be entering a manic phase with the same hyperactivity, flight-of-ideas, and delusional thinking that preceded his knocking down and kicking Mr. Rhemic. The aide said that Mr. Dewitt said he would "punch Billy's lights out." He recommends that Mr. Dewitt be put in the restrictive area for a while.

Second social worker: What did the psychiatrist say we should do?

First social worker: She said that she saw Mr. Dewitt two weeks ago in an interview, and Mr. Dewitt did not appear assaultive then. She said to hold off on use of the restrictive area.

Second social worker: I guess she's right. A psychiatrist trained at the Menninger Clinic ought to know best.

3. *One psychologist to another:* From what I can see, focused casework seemed more effective than play therapy for helping child-abusing families in one study, which I have just read. Here's its summary:

> Two contrasting therapies for the treatment of child abuse were compared in a randomized design: a focused casework approach (FCW) on the whole family and a structured play therapy (SPT) approach to the child. The Patterson coding system was used as an outcome measure to assess family interaction. There was a high drop-out rate in both groups, but of those who completed the treatment, there was a greater improvement in the focused casework group on some comparisons made. (Nicol, Smith, Kay, Hall, Barlow, & Williams, 1988).

4. *Situation:* Case conference at a mental health clinic:

    Sandra: I am concerned that we may be overusing the Borderline Personality Diagnosis (BPD) when we assess our clients. We might be using BPD as a catch-all category.

    Diana: We may be overusing the category, but I am reasonably sure that DSM-IV criteria are so specific that we can apply tighter assessment criteria for BPD with good inter-rater agreement. A meta-analysis of studies by Grueneich done in 1992 found a median Kappa inter-rater reliability for BPD of .78. I bet we could tighten our criteria and get good agreement among our workers. This of course does not address concerns about the validity of this classification, as Kirk and Kutchins point out in *The Selling of DSM.*

    Lizzie [whispering in Polly's ear]: There goes Diana again. She's a real genie-ass isn't she!

    Polly [whispering back]: She even looks like Einstein—those cowlicks in her hair make her hair pouf out all over. She looks like some dog licked her head.

*5. *Situation:* Discussion of whether to release a client from an inpatient psychiatric facility:

    Clinical psychologist: I don't know if Mr. Myers should be released so early. I am concerned that, now that his depression is lifting, he may still have great potential for suicide.

    Social worker [interrupting]: I noted that Mr. Myers cracked a joke in group this morning.

    Nurse: Yes, I recall the joke. It was something about how the president's great expectation had unraveled into great expectorations.

6. *Situation:* Juvenile court worker talking to her supervisor:

   Juvenile court worker: I'm excited! I just read a study that suggests that early intervention may substantially reduce the number of kids needing institutional placement (Kagan, Reid, Roberts, & Silverman-Pollow, 1987). The study did not involve random assignment, but maybe we could conduct a randomized trial here for some of our clients. We could offer more intensive services to some clients and standard services to others, then compare the outcome.

   Supervisor: May I be frank with you, Mary Jo? I think that because women generally are so likely to be led by their sympathies and emotions, you should keep us out of the practice-research business. Women rarely make good researchers because they lack the predisposition to objectivity that men have.

7. *Social worker speaking at a county human-services policy meeting:* Most agencies have moved to family-based treatment, but we still use the agency-based model. Don't you think we should get with it and adopt a model that is used by most other service departments?

*8. *Situation:* Case conference at a protective service agency:

Chairperson: The Armejo Family presents us with a dilemma: Should we conduct an investigation for potential child abuse or not?

Polly: As I understand the circumstances of the situation, we are in a gray area. A friend of one of their neighbors said that the neighbor said they heard children screaming and worried that the children might be abused. I understand that the family has undergone some hard times lately. The father, a custodian at a local Air Force base, has been laid off from work. We have a report from a fellow worker at the base, who is now employed, that the Armejos are having marital difficulties.

Jennifer: I am uncomfortable with initiating an investigation for child abuse on the basis of such shaky evidence. I think we should do nothing at this time. What do you think? We must investigate the abuse or leave the family alone—which is it?

*9. *Situation:* A county board meeting:

Jenny: My staff and I have conducted a survey of Hmong families here in Davis County to determine their service need. We obtained a list of families from county census records and records kept by the Hmong Mutual Assistance Organization (HMAO). Fifty-seven Hmong families live in the county, a total of 253 persons. With the help of an HMAO interpreter, we asked two head persons from each family about their needs. You have the interview guide before you that we used in the survey. In that interview we asked them to rank their needs from most important to least important. As a result, their most pressing need is . . .

Board member [speaking softly to his neighbor]: Jenny seems to have done her homework, but I don't agree with her assessment of the situation. Remember Dr. Morrison, who spoke for an hour to us about the needs of Hmong communities? I place much more confidence in Dr. Morrison's conclusions. Dr. Morrison is more widely known on this topic.

10. All staff in the Methodist Hospital Social Service Department are female. Members of the Department will interview three job candidates, one of whom is male.

   One staff member to another as they walk down the hall: Just between you and me, I think that male social workers are out of their element in hospital social work. They lack the sensitivity, empathy, and patience that it requires to do our job well. I am not at all optimistic about our male candidate's ability to do the job.

*11. *Situation:* Discussion among alcohol and other drug-abuse counselors:

   Richard: Finney and Moos (1986, p. 132) think the best hope for improving services for alcohol-dependent persons is to classify alcoholics systematically into types and to match each type with its most effective treatment. They discuss studies where there were interactions between treatment and type for mean level of sobriety, but no differences for mean success levels across treatments. What do you think about this?

   Onesmo: The idea that alcoholics are all unique (each one is different) seems wrong to me. If they were all unique, how would they all experience the same physiological symptoms of withdrawal after they have built up a tolerance for alcohol?

12. *Comment in an interdisciplinary case conference:* I notice attention deficit disorder more and more frequently in records from children referred to us. Perhaps we should classify our children into this category more often.

*13. *Situation:* An interdisciplinary case conference in a nursing home:

    Social work trainee: I don't think you should use those feeding and exercise procedures for Mrs. Shore. They don't work. Since she has Parkinson's she'll often spill her food. I also don't think you should walk her forcefully up and down the hall for exercise. A study by Rosal (1978) goes against everything you're doing in this regard.

    Nurse: You're just wet behind the ears.

*14. *Situation:* Two medical social workers are attending a professional conference. Their agency has sent them to the conference for continuing education. There are about one hundred people attending the two-day conference, for which all have paid the fifty-dollar fee:

    First social worker [whispering in friend's ear]: I wonder if this concrete imaging method really affects the longevity of cancer patients, and what kind of evidence these presenters might be able to give us.

    Second social worker: Why don't you ask the presenter?

    First social worker: I'm not comfortable enough to ask. They might all stare at me like I came from Mars.

*15. *Situation:* Two persons attending a conference on validation therapy as a method for treating confused elderly:

    First nurse: I wonder if validation therapy really helps the aged to become more oriented to time, place, and person?

    Second nurse: You'll enjoy this presentation by Diggelman this afternoon. He presents reality therapy so well that the time will just fly. Diggelman is such a sincere fellow—he isn't that hard to look at either—and he gets the audience involved in learning. He walks down into the audience and jokes with us right after the breaks. His enthusiasm gets our blood circulating again. I think that anyone so sincere and enthusiastic must be telling the truth about validation therapy.

*16. *Situation:* Confrontation between supervisor and worker:

    Supervisor [to worker]: You're late for work.

    Worker: So, you're telling me that Bill saw me come in late. I don't think it is ethical to have one worker report on another.

17. *Psychiatrist says to himself at a team meeting:* Oh no! Here comes Ms. Carey again. She's well prepared and knows the evidence about teen suicide, but I know I'll go to sleep when she starts talking. Her monotone and soft voice put me out every time.

*18. *Situation:* Judge consulting with a social worker:

    Judge Calhoun: The Chicago Police have referred a family to social services. The police found the parents and their two children living in their car without food, adequate clothing—and it's November! Which should we do, put the children in foster care or leave the family alone to fend for itself?

    Social worker: I think that in such a situation, I would have to place the children in foster care.

19. *Agency head at an agency director's meeting:* There have been a lot of conferences and presentations about methods to elicit and model expert clinical decision making and judgment. I think that we should send some of our workers to an upcoming conference on the topic. We wouldn't want to be left out of the movement.

*20. *Situation:* Case conference at a juvenile court probation agency:

   Ron: This boy has committed a very dangerous act. He constructed an explosive device and set it off in the field next to town. There wasn't anyone, other than the stone deaf, who didn't hear the boom!

   Jonathan: Yes, that's true, but he has no prior delinquent act on his record.

   Ron: We have to either place the child in juvenile detention to protect society or just let him off. Which is it?

*21. *Situation:* Case conference regarding juvenile court clients:

   Gloria: The Einhorn boys were apprehended for vandalism again. They let the dogs out of the local dog pound, rewired the back of the high-school athletic field scoreboard, monkeyed with the controls on the dam, and took a sledge hammer to Mr. Winters's old car out in the woods in the back forty acres of his farm. I plan to draw up a bar chart to indicate in dollars the total value for all that vandalism. Then we'll work on restitution to repay the victims until the chart is filled in completely. What do you think of the bar chart for restitution and goal setting?

   Albert: You know, that Winters is a con artist. I bet he claimed that the old wreck of a car in his woods is worth what a rolling vehicle would be.

   Sandy: I don't know. Some of those old vehicles are worth a lot to collectors these days. I heard of a '49 Ford that went for $15,000, and that was three years ago.

*22. *Situation:* Child Protective Service case conference:

    Mike: A police officer and I interviewed Janie, aged three, four times at Sunnyside Day Care Center. We used anatomically correct dolls to get her story. The officer and I became more and more certain with each interview that Janie has been sexually abused by one of the staff at Sunnyside.

    Antonio: I have read research by Stephen Ceci indicating that small children, especially if interviewed repeatedly, may construct an untrue story. They reported that 38% of the children who went to the doctor for a routine examination in which no pelvic examination was done reported that their genitals were touched. In successive interviews with the same children, the children have successively more elaborate descriptions of acts that the doctor did not perform. I am worried that the same thing might have occurred here. Is there any clue in the progression of her ideas, from interview to interview, that Janie might have picked up unintentional cues to shape her story?

    Mike: Your saying that I would intentionally mislead a child into giving false testimony is ridiculous. I would never help a child to lie.

23. *Faculty member speaking in a meeting in a medical school:* Simulation and gaming are used ever more frequently in schools of social work across the country to teach critical-thinking skills. We should use simulation and gaming with our students to teach difficult-to-master critical-thinking skills.

FOLLOW-UP QUESTION

Do any of this game's vignettes reflect real situations particularly well? Which one(s)?

_____

_____

_____

Exercise 9

REASONING-IN-PRACTICE GAME C: COGNITIVE BIASES IN PRACTICE

PURPOSE

To learn to identify and avoid common cognitive biases that influence practice beliefs and actions.

BACKGROUND

Practice reasoning, or clinical reasoning, refers to the process by which practitioners define problems and make decisions about what to do to help. Practitioners make decisions about what kind of data to collect, how to organize and integrate it, and what intervention methods to use. For example, a child-care worker may have to decide whether to leave a child in a foster home for another six months or return the child to its father. The child-care worker will have to decide what factors to consider when making this decision. Factors may include characteristics of the child as well as those of the father and the environment in which he lives. Such factors may include results of past placements and visits with the father. The child-care worker might review characteristics that have been found to be associated with placement outcome before making a decision.

Until fairly recently, how practitioners and clinicians made such life-affecting decisions was pretty much a mystery (Elstein, 1989, p. 287). In 1978, Elstein and his colleagues reported the first systematic study of decision making by physicians. Additional research on social judgments and the kinds of errors that occur was summarized by Nisbett and Ross in 1980 in their book *Human Inference* (see also Baron,1994). Dawes, Faust, and Meehl (1989) have compared the predictive accuracy of clinicians with actuarial methods. There are now over 140 studies showing that the latter means is more accurate for making many kinds of judgments (Dawes, 1994a). (For reviews of clinical reasoning research, see for example Corcoran & Tanner, 1988; Fonteyn, 1991; Schwartz & Griffin, 1986; Tanner, 1987).

Research related to clinical reasoning highlights many common biases and errors that can lead us astray. These reasoning patterns have also been called *heuristics, rules of thumb, habits of mind,* or *strategies for simplification* (e.g., Tversky & Kahneman, 1974). Although some strategies may work for you at times (enhance the soundness of your decisions), they can also backfire, leading to incorrect judgments and decisions (Gambrill, 1990, 1994; Weist, Finney, & Ollendick, 1992). The vignettes in Game C illustrate misleading heuristics and cognitive biases.

INSTRUCTIONS

1. Review the instructions that precede Exercise 7 before playing this game.
2. Read the description of each fallacy.
3. Read each vignette aloud when playing the game. Act out starred (*) items (see Exhibit 9.5).

DEFINITIONS, EXAMPLES, AND COUNTERMEASURES

1. *Hindsight Bias:* **the tendency to remember successful predictions of client behavior and to forget or ignore unsuccessful predictions** (Fischhoff, 1975; Fischhoff & Beyth, 1975).

   The person taken in by this bias develops a false sense of predictive accuracy. "People who know the nature of events falsely overestimate the probability with which they would have predicted it" (Dawes, 1988, p. 119). Those who fall prey to hindsight bias will often say, "I told you so!" or "Wasn't I right?" But they will not say, "I told you this would be true. I was wrong." Hindsight bias may result in unfairly blaming yourself or other practitioners for not predicting a tragic client outcome (murder, suicide, return to drug abuse). You review the person's history, searching especially for something you "should have noticed," and then hold yourself (or someone else) responsible for not taking timely action, all the while ignoring cases where the same behaviors occurred, unaccompanied by the tragic outcome.

   Example:

   First casework supervisor: That story about the client who shot his wife, his children, and then himself was a tragic one.

   Second casework supervisor: Yes, I understand that he had attempted suicide once prior to his rampage. Wouldn't you think his caseworker would have noted this and had him hospitalized?

   Countermeasures: When looking back, people tend to overestimate the accuracy of their predictions. Keep records of your predictions as you make them, not after the fact; you can also consult studies that assess risk (Hogarth, 1987).

2. *Fundamental Attribution Error:* **the tendency to attribute behavior to enduring qualities (personal traits) that are considered typical of an individual rather than to the particular situation (environment) in which they find themselves** (Kahneman, Slovic, & Tversky, 1982). In practice, this results in blaming the client, rather than identifying and altering environmental events related to problems and outcomes.

   Example: A family therapist says, "I know that the couple has faced severe financial hardships because of the husband's being laid off, the flood destroying much of their furniture and household goods, and the wife's illness and surgery, but I still think that their personality clash explains their problem. He is aggressive and she has a passive personality."

Countermeasures: Always ask, "Are there environmental variables that may influence this problem?" The environments in which we live influence our behavior. Mirowsky and Ross (1989) make a persuasive argument that psychological problems such as depression are often related to stressful environmental circumstances, including discrimination and oppression. Resolve to see clients as part of a system that includes environmental stresses. Practice models that emphasize the role of the environment include contextual and ecological models (see for example, Gambrill [in press] and Garbarino, 1992).

3. *Framing Effects:* **posing a decision in a certain way influences one's decisions. For example. framing a decision in a way that emphasizes potential benefits increases the likelihood that the decision maker will say "yes."** Conversely, the decision maker is more likely to say "no" when the decision is posed in a way that emphasizes possible negatives (Dawes, 1988, pp. 34–36). Framing effects are more powerful where life-affecting decisions are being made (e.g., whether to undergo a complex surgical procedure). Please examine Willard's predicament in Exhibit 9.1. He has said "yes" to a question posed to him that emphasized the positive aspect of a potentially life-affecting decision.

   Example:

   Counselor: Perhaps I can help you with your decision. We know that two-thirds of those who get treatment at Anderson Hospital for the Chemically Dependent remain chemical-free for two years. We also know that one-third of those treated at Luther Hospital's Chemical Dependency Unit return to chemicals within two years.

   Client: I think I'll choose Anderson because, from what you have said, my chances seem better there.

   Countermeasures: Describe negative as well as positive consequences for all alternatives.

4. *Availability:* **the tendency to make judgments based on the accessibility of concepts/events/memories—how easy it is to think/see/hear them. For example, the probability of an event is often judged by how easy it is to recall it.** People judge events to be more likely if they are vivid, recent, familiar, or have for some other reason caught their attention.

   Example: An average citizen says, "I never realized how widespread child abuse was until I heard about the Higgins case. That poor kid was so badly burned by his mother that he had to be hospitalized for three months. The reporter said the child's skin grafts had to come from a square foot of the child's buttocks and thighs, and the poor child had painful infections at the burn sites."

   Countermeasures: Try to think of alternatives that do not come to mind readily. When possible, consult surveys that describe the relative frequencies of events (see Arkes, 1981).

Exhibit 9.1

Willard's decision to take a 1% chance to live rather than face a 1% risk of dying in bed.

5. *Overlooking Regression Effects:* **ignoring the tendency for people with very high or very low scores on a measure or variable to have scores closer to the center or mean of the distribution when measured a second time.** For example, an individual who scores very low or high on some assessment measure or test is given a treatment to improve performance. If the client's posttest score is different, the regression fallacy lies in assuming that the treatment accounts for the change. Extreme pretest results tend to contain large components of error that diminish at posttest. Consider an average student who took a test and got one of the lowest scores in the class. In subsequent testing, the student will probably do better (regress toward the mean or average). Why? Perhaps during the pretest the student was ill or distracted by some problem, failed to understand the

Exhibit 9.2

Rad developed a chicken detector that worked with astounding accuracy.

instructions, or didn't see the items on the back of the last page. The test may have included questions about content in the one area he or she did not study.

The same principle holds for extremely high scores on a pretest that may have been due to unusually effective guessing or chance study of just the right topics for the test. Regression can account for the apparent effectiveness or ineffectiveness of programs designed to help those who pretest unusually low or high in some characteristic.

Example: A school social worker says, "We pretested all the fifth graders at Lowell Middle School on social skills, then involved the 10% who scored lowest in a five-week Working Together Program. This program models better social skills and provides practice for all participants. At posttest, the fifth graders scored much higher on the same measure of social skills. This program seems to work."

Countermeasures: Be wary of studies that single out extreme groups for observation. One way to avoid the regression error is to submit half the extreme group to treatment, the other half to an alternate treatment or none; then posttest both groups and compare them.

6. *Ignoring Prevalence Rate:* **the mistaken belief that the same assessment or screening tool will identify individuals just as well in a low prevalence group (where few people have the problem) as it will in a high prevalence group (where many people have the problem).** In Exhibit 9.2, the base rate for chickens is astronomical. In Exhibit 9.3, the base rate for chickens is much lower.

Example: A mental health worker says, "Did you know that

among those hospitalized for a serious mental illness (high prevalence group) who took a Suicide Prediction Instrument (SPI), 10% of those who scored in the high risk category committed suicide within two years of their release from the hospital? If we administer SPI to all the outpatient mental-health clients (low prevalence) at the Apple Valley Clinic, we can be sure that if a client scores as high risk on SPI, then that client has a 10% chance of committing suicide in the next two years."

Countermeasures: Though the mathematics to illustrate clearly why this is true can occupy a whole chapter (Gibbs, 1991, p. 217–237), Exhibits 9.2 and 9.3 quickly show the implications of base rate (proportion of the group who have a given characteristic or problem that we want to identify). In Exhibit 9.2, those to be identified comprise a large proportion *with* the characteristic (being a chicken) so identifying them is easy. In Exhibit 9.3, those to be identified consist of a very few among a varied group (Mixed Bird Aviary), so identifying them is much harder. In the low base-rate situation, there will be many more false positives (persons judged to have the problem who do not) than in the high base-rate situation.

7. ***The Law of Small Numbers: the belief that because a person has intimate knowledge of one or a few cases, he or she knows what is generally true about clients.*** This fallacy involves an insensitivity to sample size (mistakenly placing greater confidence in conclusions based on a small sample than on a much larger one) (Abraham & Schultz, 1984; Nisbett,

Exhibit 9.3

But Rad's detector failed miserably elsewhere

Borgida, Crandall, & Reed, 1982). The misleading law of small numbers is the reverse of the logically and empirically based *law of large numbers,* which states that as samples include successively larger proportions of a population, the characteristics of the sample more accurately represent the characteristics of the population (Hays, 1981). In other words, many observations provide the basis for more accurate generalizations.

Example: A child-care worker says, "Thanks for summarizing the study of 421 children that reported significantly lower intelligence among children whose mothers drank three drinks per day (Streissguth, Barr, Sampson, Darby, & Martin, 1989), but I doubt those findings. My sister regularly drank more than three drinks a day, and her children are fine."

Countermeasures: Give greater weight to conclusions based on randomly drawn, representative samples; give less weight to experience with a few clients.

8. ***Gambler's Fallacy:*** **the mistaken belief that in a series of independent events, where a run of the same event occurs, the next event is almost certain to break the run because that event is "due"** (Dawes, 1988, pp. 291–292; Hogarth, 1987, pp. 15–16). For example, if you toss a coin fairly, and four heads appear, then you tend to believe that the next coin tossed should be a tail because the tail is "about due" to even things out.

Example: "My husband and I have just had our eighth child. Another girl, and I am really disappointed. I suppose I should thank God she was healthy, but this one was supposed to have been a boy. Even the doctor told me that the law of averages were [sic] in our favor 100 to 1" ("Dear Abby," June 28, 1974; cited in Dawes, 1988, p. 275). The doctor's advice was in error, because on the eighth trial, the chance was essentially .5, as it was for the other births. "Like coins, sperm have no memories, especially not for past conceptions of which they know nothing" (Dawes, 1988, p. 291).

Countermeasures: Remember that for truly independent events —tosses of a fair coin, birth of boy or girl in a given hospital— what happened previously cannot affect the next in the series. No matter how many times you enter the lottery, your chances of winning the next time you play will be the same no matter how many times you have played in the past. This is important to understand and to convey to those clients who spend money they can ill afford on gambling.

9. ***Anchoring and Insufficient Adjustment:*** **the tendency to base estimates of the likelihood of events on an initial piece of information and then not adjust this estimate in the face of new and vital information** (Tversky & Kahneman, 1982). There are several reasons for anchoring, including the order in which information is given, and the tendency of observers to overestimate or underestimate probabilities (Tversky & Kahneman, 1982).

Example:

Intake Worker: I always base decisions about a client's chances for rehabilitation on my first few moments with the client.

Countermeasures: Use strategies that encourage you to entertain alternative hypotheses. For example, when you begin a group meeting, you could resolve to consider several hypotheses about what may be the principal interest of the group at the meeting. Resolve not to form an opinion until each member of the group has had a chance to speak. Also, you could select a hypothesis "at the other end of the pole," or that directly counters your initial estimate or belief.

10. *Nonfallacy Items:* **items that do not contain fallacies.** These items illustrate examples of persons who use sound premises to reach a conclusion about the effectiveness of a treatment or what is generally true of clients. Nonfallacy items also show someone pointing out or avoiding a fallacy.

Refer to Exhibit 9.4 as needed when playing Game C.

Exhibit 9.4

Fallacies in Game C

No.	Name
1.	**Hindsight Bias**
2.	**Fundamental Attribution Error**
3.	**Framing Effects**
4.	**Availability**
5.	**Overlooking Regression Effects**
6.	**Ignoring Prevalence Rate**
7.	**The Law of Small Numbers**
8.	**Gambler's Fallacy**
9.	**Anchoring and Insufficient Adjustment**
10.	**Nonfallacy Item**

Exhibit 9.5   **VIGNETTES FOR GAME C:**
COGNITIVE BIASES IN PRACTICE

Your Name   Date
_____

Course
_____

Instructor's Name
_____

REMINDER

We think that the starred (*) items work best if the narrator reads the background and several actors act out the parts. Acting out the situation vividly portrays the content of each vignette. We hope this active participation will help you to retain the lesson in memory and transfer new knowledge and skills to practice. Again, consult the general instructions for playing the Reasoning-in-Practice Games. Consult Exhibit 9.4 as needed.

*1. *Situation:* A new supervisor has just been hired as an early childhood/special education director. The school administration is concerned that too many children who don't need special education are admitted into the school's special education program; then, in the spring when the program fills, too few children are admitted into the program who really need it.

New supervisor: I think that we need to administer standardized tests to see which children should be admitted into the new program.

First special-education teacher: We haven't used standardized tests before, and we have done a good job of identifying those needing the program. Think for example of the Williams boy. We admitted him, and he clearly needs our services.

Second special-education teacher: Yes! And there's the Gordan girl, and she clearly needed speech therapy.

*2. *Situation:* School officials have requested a study to evaluate their district's preschool enrichment program. The child-care worker responsible for the study is reporting.

Child-care worker: We administered the Bailey's Developmental Inventory to all four-year-old children in the Washington County School District. Those who scored in the lowest 5% were enrolled in the District's Preschool Enrichment Program. The children in the Enrichment Program scored 25% higher one year later, just prior to kindergarten.

School official: The Enrichment Program really helps preschool kids approach the average level for children starting kindergarten.

*3. *Situation:* Orthopedic surgeon speaking to his patient:

Doctor: If you have orthoscopic surgery on your knee, you will have a good chance for full use of your knee.

Patient: How good a chance?

Doctor: In about 75% of such cases, the operation is a complete success.

Patient: And what about with cortisone treatment?

Doctor: About a quarter of those who get cortisone do not improve to full use of the knee.

Patient: Let's do the knee surgery.

*4. *Situation:* Two social workers are discussing the grade-school performance of children from a local low-income housing area.

Maria: Remember that envelope full of paint chips that I sent to the county health department? I got the chips off the window sills and floors of the tenement housing on Bridge Street. The county health nurse called today to tell me that the paint chips are toxic—full of lead! The nurse said that anyone breathing dust from the paint or ingesting food contaminated with the lead, or infants and toddlers eating the chips as they crawl around the floor, could suffer long-term cognitive deficits and other health problems (Berkow & Fletcher, 1987).

Joe: I was a little worried about that as a factor in school performance. Still, I think that the major determinant of performance is cultural: The Bridge Street people just don't value education. They are simply not motivated enough to do anything about education in their area.

5. *Nurse:* I recall quite vividly a homosexual that I referred for counseling just a month ago. The poor fellow's personal and professional life caused such stress that he came in complaining of stomach pains that frequently awakened him at two in the morning. His pain was relieved by food. He said that he felt isolated and alone working at a military base, and he was afraid that his co-workers would find out about his homosexuality. I guess being homosexual must be quite stressful for most homosexuals.

6. *Medical social worker:* I have looked for evidence and counter-evidence, and the best I could find supports the value of patient education. Scalzi, Burke, and Greenland (1980) did an objective review and conducted a study to evaluate the effects of patient education on heart-attack patients, specifically, their knowledge of their disease, compliance with their medical treatment, and survival rate. Scalzi and her colleagues found no difference in survival rate between nineteen in their treatment program and thirteen in a nontreated comparison group, but the treatment group knew more about the disease and complied more with treatment in the following areas: medications, physical activity, resumption of sexual activity, weight reduction, and treatment and reporting of chest pain and shortness of breath (p. 853). In the absence of counterevidence, which I looked for, I plan to support patient-education programs.

*7. *Situation:* Two alcohol and drug abuse counselors are talking in their office over a bag lunch.

    Maureen: Who would have thought that Rodrigues would be first among the eight in the recovery group to start using drugs again?

    Penny: Oh, it didn't surprise me. There was something about him that tipped me off. I still can't put my finger on it. But I would have guessed it.

8. *Client:* I'd much rather take a long shot (10%) chance to overcome the problem than face a likely failure (90%).

9. *School social worker:* Your study of fifty high-school boys that found no relationship between level of knowledge learned in a sex education program and more permissive attitudes toward sex does not impress me (Hoch, 1971). I know a student at King High School who took the same kind of program who swore that his permissiveness began because of it. He just found out that he has AIDS, and he has transmitted it to at least one female student.

10. *Social-work supervisor:* We arranged that all 100 social workers employed by Megalopolis County would take the State Social Work Competency Examination. The top ten were given engraved gold plaques with their name on them for their offices. During the year immediately after the examination, we arranged a series of in-service training programs for all 100. Then we administered the same examination to all 100 a year later. Much to our surprise, the top ten on the prior test averaged 12% worse on their second test. These top ten must have relaxed during the training and not paid much attention.

*11. *Situation:* Two girls-club leaders are talking about Kisha, a new club member.

    Ginny: I don't think Kisha is going to graduate from Washington High School. Both of Kisha's parents are illiterate. Her father is absent from the home. Her mother is on AFDC. Her school is notorious for not graduating its students. She's attractive and bright, but there are pimps in her neighborhood.

    Pat: Yes. I don't think she has the strength of character needed to stay with her studies.

12. *Caseworker planning to visit an Aid-for-Dependent-Children case in a dangerous area of the city:* Three from our office have gotten through to their cases with backup support in the past with only minor confrontations: I'm sure the next one will have trouble.

*13. *Situation:* A researcher is describing a risk-assessment instrument to an audience of protective-service workers.

    Researcher: My child-abuse prediction instrument accurately identified 90% of protective-service clients who reabused their child within a year.

    Protective-service worker: Wow! If we could administer your test to all families in the community, we could identify 90% there, too.

14. *Surgeon:* I evaluated a seventy-eight-year-old man for lethargy, stomach pain, and sleep disturbance after he retired and his wife died. I conducted elaborate and costly tests over the course of a year to investigate physiological causes, including lung cancer, thyroid disease, and an infection of the stomach and intestines. I didn't think to investigate depression as a psychiatric condition (see such a case in Kassirer & Kopelman, 1991, pp. 242–247).

15. *Caseworker:* Typically, when I have a little information about the client, I find that no amount of additional history taking and information from other sources can change my mind about what to do.

*16. *Situation:* Two university instructors discussing teaching over their lunch break:

   First instructor: I can tell on the first day of class who the stars will be. The star students just shine out somehow.

   Second instructor: I think you might be guilty of forming an initial opinion hastily, then not revising your opinion as the semester wears on. I would be worried also about bias in grading if you're not careful.

17. *Hospital social worker:* I try to get a good look at an aged patient's chart before seeing the patient. Usually, all I need to know about whether the patient should be discharged to a community program, a nursing home, or some other program, is right in the chart.

*18. *Situation:* Two psychologists discussing how to help poor readers in an elementary school.

First child psychologist: I have some information that might help your poor reader and his parents. Miller, Robson, and Bushell (1986) studied thirty-three failing readers and their parents. The children were ages eight to eleven and had reading delays of at least eighteen months. The parents read with their kids over six weeks for an average of 7.6 hours per family. Reading accuracy and comprehension scores for the paired-reading-program kids were compared with those of kids who did not participate in the program. Results favored kids in the program. You might try paired reading.

Second child psychologist: About a year ago, one of our psychologists tried paired reading. The reading developed into a battle ground. The kid bugged his parents constantly while they tried to read with him. The kid was real innovative when it came to distractions during the paired reading: He ate a goldfish. I don't think I'll try paired reading.

19. *One probation officer to another:* My most recent three sex offenders have been apprehended for a new offense within two months of when their cases were assigned to me. This next one is bound to be a success.

*20. *Situation:* A corrections policy maker is telling an audience about a new instrument to predict outcome for parolees (*parole* is a conditional release from prison; *probation* is a suspended prison sentence to be served in the community provided that the probationer follows certain rules).

    Corrections policy maker: Our parole-prediction study found that 95% of criminal offenders who scored in the high-risk group and were released from our maximum security prison went on to commit a new offense within a year.

    Community probation officer: I would like to give your parole-prediction measure to my clients so I can identify high-risk clients, too. I'll be able to tell the judge in my presentence report which offenders should be handled more conservatively.

FOLLOW-UP QUESTION

Do any of this game's vignettes reflect real situations particularly well? Which one(s)?

_____

_____

_____

_____

_____

_____

Exercise 10
PREPARING A FALLACIES
FILM FESTIVAL

PURPOSE

1. To help you to become intimate with a practice fallacy that you and a partner have chosen to demonstrate before the class in a brief vignette.
2. To learn more about other fallacies by watching others demonstrate theirs.

BACKGROUND

The credit for devising an exercise in which professionals *purposefully* mess up for instructional purposes may go to clinical scholars at the University of North Carolina (Michael, Boyce, & Wilcox, 1984, p. xi). Apparently, a clinical scholars' skit in "Clinical Flaw Catching" left such an impression on Max Michael and his colleagues that they wrote the delightful book, *Biomedical Bestiary,* complete with humorous illustrations of thirteen fallacies from the medical literature.

In this exercise, student presentations will illustrate each fallacy, much as the images in *Biomedical Bestiary* do.

INSTRUCTIONS

1. Sign up with a partner for one practice fallacy from the List of Practice Fallacies and Pitfalls at the end of this exercise (Exhibit 10.1). These fallacies are defined in the Reasoning-in-Practice Games and in the professional literature.
2. Read about your chosen fallacy (see References at the back of this workbook) and note down important points. Track down references to additional literature cited in sources that you locate. Keep a record of sources by noting complete references for each one. We favor the American Psychological Association's reference style (APA style) used in this workbook. A librarian should be able to help you to find additional material about practice fallacies in books on critical thinking, *Psychological Abstracts* (PsychLit), *Index Medicus* (Medline), and *Social Work Abstracts* (SWAB).
3. First, in no more than two pages, define the fallacy, using literature to document your definition, and describe how you would avoid the fallacy in practice situations. You may use conceptual

definitions, examples, or even measures to define your fallacy. Second, attach a reference list using APA style. Third, attach a script for actors to follow, including descriptions of props (see Exhibit 10.2 for a sample vignette script). Your vignette should last, at most, about a minute. Vignettes seem to work best if they are brief (about 30 seconds), are a bit overdone, make use of props, and clearly demonstrate just *one* fallacy.

4. Demonstrate your chosen fallacy to the class with your partner or with help from other students whom you direct. (They'll volunteer because they'll probably need help with *their* vignettes.) Your demonstration should include a short introductory statement describing who is involved, where it takes place, and what is going on so that your audience can get the gist of what they will see. Your vignette can either be highly realistic or be overacted and humorous, with overdressing, engaging props, or eccentric mannerisms. Your instructor may ask for your permission to videotape your skits so they can be reviewed.

FOLLOW-UP QUESTION

What have you learned from this exercise?

_____

_____

_____

_____

_____

_____

_____

_____

_____

_____

_____

_____

_____

_____

_____

Exhibit 10.1

List of Practice Fallacies and Pitfalls*

1. Manner, Style, Charisma, Stage Presence
2. New, Newness, Tried-and-True, Tradition
3. Uncritical Documentation, Relying on Citation Alone
4. Ad Hominem, Focusing on the Person (Attack, Praise) Rather Than Argument
5. Appeal to Experience, All Evidence Is Equally Good, Experience
6. Popularity, Peer Pressure, Bandwagon, Appeal to Numbers, Because Everybody . . .
7. Ad Verecundium, Appeal to Authority, Status, Titles, Degrees
8. Lack of Objectivity, Not Objective, Bias, Vested Interest
9. Either-Or, Only Two Sides, Only Two Alternatives, False Dilemma
10. Testimonial
11. Hasty Generalization, Biased Sample, Sweeping Generalization
12. Vagueness, Unclear Term, Undefined Term, Vague Outcome Criterion
13. Case Example
14. Two Questions, Double-Barreled Question, Two-Headed, Ambiguous, Bipolar Question
15. Leading, Loaded, Biased Question
16. Tautology, Word Defines Itself
17. Post Hoc, Post Hoc Ergo Propter Hoc, After This, After This Therefore Because of This, Temporal Order
18. Jargon
19. Overlooking Regression Effects, Regression to the Mean, Regression Fallacy
20. Ignoring Base Rate, Ignoring Prior Probability, Ignoring Prevalence Rate
21. Selection Bias, Biased Selection of Clients
22. Soft-Hearted Therefore Soft-Headed
23. Focusing on Successes Only
24. Diversion, Red Herring, Drawing a Red Herring Across the Trail of an Argument
25. Stereotyping
26. Groupthink
27. Straw Man Argument
28. Hindsight Bias, I Knew It Would Be So, Hindsight Does Not Equal Foresight, False Memory
29. Fundamental Attribution Error
30. Framing Effects
31. Availability, Ignorance of Availability, Ignoring Availability
32. The Law of Small Numbers
33. Gambler's Fallacy
34. Anchoring and Insufficient Adjustment, Anchoring, Anchoring Effect

*Defined in Reasoning-in-Practice Games, Professional Thinking Forms' key, Principles of Reasoning, Inference, and Decision Making key, and professional literature.

Exhibit 10.2 **SAMPLE VIGNETTE SCRIPT**

FOCUSING ON SUCCESSES ONLY

by Michael Werner and Tara Lehman
University of Wisconsin, Eau Claire

Situation: Four patients sit bedraggled with spots painted on their faces.

[Hold up a sign that reads "9:00 A.M."]

Doctor: Today we are trying an experimental drug for people such as yourselves, who have blotchy skin disease. This should take care of your disease in a matter of seconds. *[Pours water into four glasses containing dry ice, i.e., solid carbon dioxide. Everybody appears to take a drink. (Don't drink, it will burn the mouth.)]*

[Hold up a sign that reads "9:01 A.M."]

Doctor [looking at first patient]: Wow! Your skin really cleared up. How do you feel?

First patient: I feel great!

Doctor: This stuff really does work: At last, a new miracle drug!

First patient [looking at the other three patients]: But what about these other three uncured, sickly, sorry-looking specimens? *[The other three hang their heads.]*

Doctor: That's OK. It doesn't matter. We did have one great success! It really works. What a breakthrough! I must tell all my colleagues to use it.

Exercise 11
FALLACY SPOTTING IN PROFESSIONAL CONTEXTS

PURPOSE

To hone your skills in spotting fallacies in professional sources.

BACKGROUND

This is one of our own students' favorite exercises. The task is to select some quote relevant to your profession and critique it (see items below). You may wish to select quotes from your professors. Or, you could critique a statement in this very book. Although we have tried hard to avoid fallacies, we are sure that we have been guilty of some. In fact, we would be delighted if you would write to us about them so we can correct them.

INSTRUCTIONS

1. Review fallacies in the Reasoning-in-Practice Games and in the Professional Thinking Form's scoring key.
2. Identify an example of professional content that you think illustrates a fallacy.
3. Note the complete source on the Fallacy Spotting in Professional Contexts Form (Exhibit 11.1) using APA reference style..
4. Give verbatim quote that states a claim (include page numbers as relevant). You could duplicate relevant portions of an article/ chapter and attach a copy highlighting the quote of concern. To be fair, do not take a sentence out of its context in a way that alters its meaning.
5. Identify (name) the fallacy involved and explain why you think it represents this fallacy in the critique section of the worksheet.

Exhibit 11.1 **FALLACY SPOTTING IN PROFESSIONAL CONTEXTS**

Your Name _____   Date _____

Course _____

Instructor's Name _____

Source*

_____

_____

_____

Claim. Give verbatim description or attach a copy noting content focused on.

_____

_____

_____

_____

Critique. Identify the main fallacy, describe why you think this applies to the quoted material, and describe possible consequences of believing an inaccurate claim. (Use extra paper as needed and attach to this form.)

_____

_____

_____

_____

FOLLOW-UP QUESTION

What have you learned from this exercise?

_____

_____

_____

_____

*If newspapers, give correct date, title of article, author, and page numbers. If journal, give title, author, volume number, and page number. If book, give full title, author, date, publisher. Use APA style. If in a conversation, describe context and position of person.

4 THINKING CRITICALLY ABOUT SPECIFIC ASSESSMENT AND INTERVENTION DECISIONS

Although educators in the helping professions encourage helpers to base practice decisions on related research, helpers often fail to do so. A review of fifteen studies in social work reported "ambivalent" attitudes toward research (Lazar, 1991, p. 34). This reluctance to consult practice-related research is seen in other professions as well. Bishop (1984), a medical educator, said that most contemporary medical students view science and medicine as "difficult allies at best" (p. 92). In their book on how to interpret the medical research literature, Michael, et al. (1984, p. ix) say, "Most medical students regard epidemiology as somewhere between mud-wrestling and mah-jongg in its relevance to medicine." Studies show that many nursing students view research as dull and of little relevance to their practice (Blenner, 1991, p. 32).

We are not saying that all, or even most, students have a negative attitude toward research; we are just saying that there is some resistance to relying on research findings and data as guides to practice. Some of the responsibility for not basing practice decisions on related research lies on the shoulders of the very educators who are concerned that practitioners do not use this knowledge. Educators may employ jargon-filled writing that is difficult to follow and fail to clearly spell out practice implications. Sometimes teachers lack skill in evaluating the quality of research as it relates to practice decisions. Other reasons include splitting research off from practice courses in professional educational programs and difficulties in getting quick access to valuable content. The exercises in Part 4 address the "So what?" and its family of related questions that students often ask about research. Exercise 12 provides guidelines for reviewing research investigating the effectiveness of practice methods. Exercise 13 provides an opportunity to consider the effects of clarity of problem definition on agreement among different raters. Exercise 14 introduces you to some common pitfalls in making predictions.

Exercise 15 provides an opportunity to consider ethical issues that arise in everyday practice based on the vignettes in Exercises 7–9. Critical thinkers raise ethical questions about commonly accepted practices, and because they value seeking the truth over following authority and dogma, they may find themselves in positions that present ethical binds. Discovering what is most ethical will often require careful consideration of the implications of different options. Exercises 16 and 17 highlight the harms that may occur because of a lack of critical thinking. Exercise 18 provides a checklist to rate plans for helping clients relative to twenty-two criteria. Exercise 19 is designed to enhance your skill in clarifying and critically examining arguments. Exercise 20 provides questions for thinking critically about case records.

Exercise 12
EVALUATING STUDY QUALITY AND TREATMENT EFFECT

PURPOSE

1. To identify the earmarks of a good treatment-evaluation study.
2. To accurately and reliably evaluate practice-related research.
3. To rate the magnitude of a treatment's effect size in two ways.

BACKGROUND

Central to critical thinking is knowing how to weigh evidence critically and fairly when you seek answers to questions. This exercise will help you answer the following questions: (1) What does this study tell me about the effectiveness of this method compared with others? (2) Which treatment helps clients the most? (3) Is one study better than another? and (4) What's a good study?

INSTRUCTIONS

Follow the next two steps.

Exhibit 12.1

Primitive practioners looking for ways to use study results

Step 1

Please spend five or ten minutes previewing the Quality of Study Rating Form in Exhibit 12.2. This form was developed to provide a standard for answering questions about the soundness of a study (Gibbs, 1991). It helps someone reviewing a study of the effectiveness of an intervention to rate the study's quality on a 100-point scale. The form also provides guidelines for rating the impact of the intervention in units that can be compared across studies.

Specifically, the Quality of Study Rating Form contains a few lines near the top for you to describe the study by noting (1) the type of client who participated (e.g., dyslexic children, aged persons with Alzheimer's disease), (2) the treatment method(s) being evaluated, (3) the most important outcome measures, and (4) the reference for the study in APA format.

Items 1–16 will help you to answer questions about the soundness of a study and how it compares with another study. A study with 80 points should provide more sound information about the causal link between treatment and outcome than one with 30. Based on hundreds of studies reviewed by our students, we have found that studies with 80 points are extremely unusual; those with 50 to 80 points constitute about the top third, and those with fewer than 40 points are the most common.

For those studies having roughly the same total quality points, Items 17 and 18 can help you to answer questions about which method helps the most. Items 17 and 18 concern the magnitude of an intervention's effectiveness in standardized units. Effect Size 1 (ES1) gets larger if one method has a greater effect than a second (or a control), given that larger numbers on the outcome measure mean greater effect. As a rough rule, a small ES1 is approximately .2, a medium one about .5, and a large one about .8 or greater (Cohen, 1977, p. 24). When Effect Size 1 approaches zero, there is essentially no difference in the relative effectiveness of the compared treatments. A method that produces a negative Effect Size 1 produces a harmful (iatrogenic) effect.

Effect Size 2 (ES2) measures the difference between the percent of subjects improved in one group compared with the percent improved in another treatment (or control group). If 30% improve in one treatment and 20% improve in the other, then their ES2 is 10% (i.e., 30% − 20% = 10%). Though Effect Size 2 is easier to interpret than Effect Size 1, many studies fail to include sufficient information to compute Effect Size 2.

Step 2

Rate the study in Exhibit 12.3 on the blank Quality of Study Rating Form in Exhibit 12.2. For greater realism, assume that you work as a medical social worker in a large hospital. You and other members of the Social Work Department have observed that patients being admitted to the hospital seem anxious and a bit bewildered by the experience. You wonder if patients would feel less anxious if they watched a brief videotape that answers common questions arising during admission. One of your colleagues has done a computer search of the *Social Work Abstracts* database and retrieved the study described in Exhibit 12.3.

Exhibit 12.2   **QUALITY OF STUDY RATING FORM (QSRF)***

Your Name _____   Date _____

Course _____

Instructor's Name _____

Client Type(s) _____

Treatment Method(s) _____

Outcome Measure to Compute ES1 _____

Outcome Measure to Compute ES2 _____

Source (APA Format) _____

_____

Criteria for Rating Study

Clear Definition of Treatment					6. Subjects randomly assigned to treatment or control (20 pts)	7. Subjects randomly selected (4 pts)	8. Nontreated control group (4 pts)
1 Who (4 pts)	2 What (4 pts)	3 Where (4 pts)	4 When (4 pts)	5 Why (4 pts)			

Criteria for Rating Study (cont.)

9. Number of subjects in smallest treatment group exceeds 20 (4 pts)	10. Outcome measure has face validity (4 pts)	11. Treatment outcome measure was checked for reliability (5 pts)	12. Reliability measure has value greater than .70 or percent of rater agreement greater than 70% (5 pts)	13. Outcome of treatment was measured after treatment was completed (4 pts)	14. Test of statistical significance was made and $p < .05$ (20 pts)

Criteria for Rating Study (cont.)   Criteria for Rating Effect Size

15. Follow-up greater than 75% (10 pts)	16. Total quality points (TQP)	17. Effect Size (ES1)	18. Effect Size (ES2)
		$$ES1 = \frac{\bar{x}_t - \bar{x}_c}{s_c} = \frac{\text{(mean of treatment)} - \text{(mean of alternate treatment or control)}}{\text{standard deviation of control or alternate treatment}}$$	$ES2 = P_t - P_c$ = (proportion improved in treatment) − (proportion improved in control group or alternate treatment)

*From "Quality of Study Rating Form: An Instrument for Synthesizing Evaluation Studies" by L. E. Gibbs, 1989, *Journal of Social Work Education*, 25(1), p. 67. Copyright 1989 by The Council on Social Work Education; adapted by permission; and from L. E. Gibbs, *Scientific Reasoning for Social Workers*, pp. 193–197, copyright 1991 by Merrill, an imprint of Macmillan Publishing Company; reprinted by permission.

Exhibit 12.2
(continued)

EXPLANATION OF CRITERIA

In the Client Type and Treatment Methods sections, state briefly and specifically what the key identifying features are for client type (e.g., adult victims of sex abuse). Also list the principal treatment method and outcome measure. Use one form for each treatment comparison.

Give either zero points or the particular point value indicated if the study meets the criterion, as numbered and described below:

1. The author describes *who* is treated by stating the subjects' average age, standard deviation of age and sex or proportion of males and females, and diagnostic category, for example, child abusers, schizophrenics.

2. The authors tell *what* the treatment involves so specifically that you could apply the treatment with nothing more to go on than their description, or they refer you to a book, videotape, or article that describes the treatment method.

3. Authors state *where* the treatment occurred so specifically that you could contact people at that facility by phone or by letter.

4. Authors tell the *when* of the treatment by stating how long subjects participated in the treatment in days, weeks, or months or tell how many treatment sessions were attended by subjects.

5. Authors either discuss a specific theory that describes *why* they used one or more treatment methods or they cite literature that supports the use of the treatment method.

6. The author states specifically that subjects were *randomly assigned* to treatment groups or refers to the assignment of subjects to treatment or control groups on the basis of a table of random numbers or other accepted randomization procedure. Randomization implies that each subject has an equal chance of being assigned to either a treatment or control group. If the author says subjects are randomly assigned but assigns subjects to treatments by assigning every other one or by allowing subjects to choose their treatment groups, subjects are not randomly assigned.

7. *Selection* of subjects is different from *random assignment*. Random selection means subjects are taken from some potential pool of subjects for inclusion in the study by using a table of random numbers or other random procedures; for example, if subjects are chosen randomly from among all residents in a nursing home, the results of the study can be generalized more confidently to all residents of the nursing home.

8. Members of the *nontreated control group* do not receive a different kind of treatment; they receive *no* treatment. An example of a nontreated control group would be a group of subjects who are denied group counseling while others are given group counseling. Subjects in the nontreated control group might receive treatment at a later date, but do not receive treatment while experimental group subjects are receiving their treatment.

9. Those in the treatment group or groups are those who receive some kind of special care intended to help them. It is this treatment that is being evaluated by those doing the study. The results of the study will state how effective the treatment or treatment groups have been when compared with each other or with a nontreated control group. In order to meet criterion 9, *the number of subjects in the largest treatment group must be at least 21.** Here, "number of subjects" means total number of individuals, not number of couples or number of groups.

---

*Not everyone would agree with this number.

Exhibit 12.2
(continued)

10. *Face validity of an outcome measure* is present if the outcome measure used to determine the effectiveness of treatment makes sense to you. A good criterion for the sense of an outcome measure is whether the measure evaluates something that should logically be affected by the treatment. For example, drinking behavior has face validity as an outcome measure for treating alcoholism. An intelligence quotient may not have face validity as an indicator for alcoholism treatment effect.

11. Some criterion or criteria must be used to measure the effectiveness of a treatment. Examples of such outcome measures might include number of days spent in the community after release from treatment before readmission, score on a symptom rating scale, or number of days after release from treatment during which no alcohol was consumed. For this criterion, it is not enough to merely state that outcome was measured in some way, the author must cite a measurement procedure or describe how the outcome was measured and evaluate the measure's reliability. *Reliability*—the consistency of measurement—is frequently measured in an outcome evaluation study by comparing the findings of investigators who independently rate the performance of individuals in treatment or nontreated control groups. Another less frequently used way to measure reliability of outcome measures is to have the same individual rate the performance of subjects and then rerate performance. In single-subject studies, two raters may rate the subject's behavior independently for cross-rater comparison.

    The reliability criterion is satisfied only if the author of the study affirms that evaluations were made of the outcome measure's reliability (for example, interrater agreement), and the *author lists a numerical value of some kind for this measure of reliability*. Where multiple outcome criteria were used, reliability checks of the major outcome criteria satisfy number 11.

12. The *reliability coefficient discussed in number 11 is .70* or greater (70% or better).

13. *At least one outcome measure was obtained after treatment was completed.* After release from the hospital, after drug therapy was completed, after subjects quit attending inpatient group therapy—all are posttreatment measures. For example, if subjects were released from the mental hospital on November 10, and some measure of success was obtained on November 11, then the study meets criterion 9. Outcome measured both during treatment and after treatment ended is sufficient to meet this criterion.

14. *Tests of statistical significance* are generally referred to by phrases such as "differences between treatment groups were significant at the .05 level" or "results show statistical significance for outcome." Give credit for meeting this criterion *only* if author refers to a test of statistical significance by name (e.g., analysis of variance, chi square, t test) *and* gives a p value, for example $p < .05$, and the p value is equal to or smaller than .05.

15. The proportion of subjects *successfully followed-up* refers to the number contacted to measure outcome compared with the number who began the experiment. To compute this proportion followed-up for each group studied (i.e., treatment group, control group), determine the number of subjects who initially entered the experiment in the group and determine the number successfully followed-up. (If there is more than one follow-up period, use the longest one.) Then for each group, divide the number

Exhibit 12.2
(continued)

successfully followed-up by the number who began in each group and multiply each quotient by 100. For example, if 20 entered a treatment group, but 15 were followed-up in that group, the result would be: $(15/20)100 = 75\%$. Compute the proportion followed-up for all groups involved in the experiment. If the *smallest* of these percentages equals or exceeds 75%, the study meets this criterion.

16. Total quality points (TQP) is simply the sum of the point values for criteria 1–15.

17. Effect size (ES1) is a number that summarizes the strength of effect of a given treatment. The index can be computed as follows:

$$ES1 = (\bar{x}_t - \bar{x}_c)/(S_c)$$

$$= \frac{\text{(mean of treatment)} - \text{(mean of control or alternate treatment group)}}{\text{standard deviation of control or alternate treatment}}$$

This formula is for computing ES1 when outcome means of treatment groups and control groups are given. To compute an effect size from information presented in an article, select two means to compare; for example, outcome might be a mean of a treatment group compared with a mean of a nontreated control group. Subtract the mean of the second group from the mean of the first group and divide this value by the standard deviation of the second group. (Standard deviations are indicated by various signs and symbols, including *s.d., S, s, SD,* or σ.) ES1 may be a negative or positive number. If the number is positive, the first group may have the greater treatment effect—this assumes that positive outcome on the outcome measure implies larger numbers on that measure. If the ES1 is negative when comparing a treatment group against a control group, the treatment may produce a harmful or iatrogenic effect. If the number is negative when comparing two alternate treatments, the first treatment is less effective than the second. The larger a positive ES1 value, the stronger the effect of treatment.

18. We can also compute ES2 for proportions or percentages, using the formula:

$$ES2 = P_t - P_c = \left(\frac{\text{number improved in treatment}}{\text{total number in treatment group}} \times 100 \right)$$

$$- \left(\frac{\text{number improved in alternate treatment or control}}{\text{total number in alternate treatment or control}} \times 100 \right)$$

Assume that we are comparing the proportion in a treatment group who are improved against the proportion in a control group who are improved. Let us say that 70% of those in the treatment group are improved and 50% of those in the control group are also improved for a particular outcome measure. ES2 then equals 70% minus 50%, or 20%. Thus, the proportion of improvement attributable to the treatment may be 20%. As a general rule, ES1 and ES2 can be interpreted with greater confidence in studies with a higher TQP. However, even in stronger studies, results may be affected by factors other than those listed in the QSRF.

Exhibit 12.3

Reproduced with permission of authors and publisher from:
Holden, G., Speedling, E., & Rosenberg, G. Evaluation of an intervention designed to improve patients'
hospital experience. *Psychological Reports,* 1992, 71, 547–550. © Psychological Reports 1992.

EVALUATION OF AN INTERVENTION DESIGNED TO IMPROVE PATIENTS' HOSPITAL EXPERIENCE[1]

Gary Holden, Edward Speedling, Gary Rosenberg

Mount Sinai School of Medicine
New York, New York

Summary.—The influence of a videotape, shown in a hospital admitting room, on patients' state anxiety and concerns about hospitalization was assessed in a preliminary study. For both state anxiety and specific concerns regarding hospitalization the pretest scores on each variable accounted for the preponderance of the variance in the posttest scores. In both instances, the intervention and the interaction of the intervention with the pretest scores accounted for less than 1% of variance in the outcome. While finding small effects to be significant for such a small sample ($N = 93$) is unlikely, the sample size was adequate to detect medium to large effects. More important was the fact that 73.33% of the videotape intervention group indicated that they did not watch the video, which leads us to the conclusion that this intervention as tested is not worthwhile.

Being admitted to a hospital is an anxiety-producing event. We were recently asked to do a preliminary study of the effect of a videotape shown in a hospital admitting room. The videotape included a role model who was depicted through a stay in this particular hospital. The videotape provided information about the process of hospitalization and showed the model encountering problems representative of typical patient concerns and finding solutions to those problems.

Gagliano (1988) reviewed studies using film or video in patient education published between 1975 and 1986 (cf. Nielsen & Sheppard, 1988). She noted that: "[a] strength of video is role-modeling. When applied to well defined, self-limited stressful situations, role modeling in video decreases patients' anxiety, pain, and sympathetic arousal while increasing knowledge, cooperation, and coping ability" (p. 785). More recent research supports the use of videotape interventions in health care settings (Allen, Danforth, & Drabman, 1989; Rasnake & Linscheid, 1989). The central question addressed by this study was whether experimental subjects would report significantly less anxiety than control subjects after viewing the videotape during the admission process.

METHOD

The State-Trait Anxiety Inventory was selected as the primary outcome measure because its psychometric properties are well-established and it has been used widely (Spielberger, 1983). Subjects completed the State anxiety scale at both pretest and posttest. They completed the Trait anxiety scale at pretest only. An additional scale was created to assess patients' concerns regarding specific aspects of hospitalization. Subjects completed this scale at both pretest and posttest. Subjects were English-speaking, nonemergency admissions to a large, urban, tertiary care medical center. Eligible consenting patients were enrolled in the admissions office, with group assignments being random. These patients completed the initial assessment battery shortly after arrival. Patients completed the second assessment in the admissions area following the admission process.

[1]The authors acknowledge the ongoing support and assistance of Robert Southwick, Erica Rubin, and the Mount Sinai Medical Center admitting room staff, in the completion of this project. Requests for reprints should be addressed to G. Holden, D.S.W., Box 1252, Mount Sinai School of Medicine, 1 Gustave L. Levy Place, New York, NY 10029-6574. Reproduced with permission of the authors and publisher.

Intervention

Initially, two versions of the intervention were employed as previous researchers found structured viewing of a videotaped intervention was superior to incidental viewing (Kleemeier & Hazzard, 1984). In the structured viewing condition subjects were taken to a quiet room and given a brief explanation of what they were about to see before actually viewing the 14-min. long videotape. In the regular viewing condition, subjects were told that this videotape about hospitalization was playing on a monitor in the corner of the room and they could watch it if they chose. This second condition represents the more pragmatic use of such an intervention given the pace in most waiting rooms.

Results

The first result was that the structured viewing condition was quickly dropped because the refusal rate was very high. Patients were unwilling to leave the admitting room, despite reassurances that staff would always know where they were and they would not 'lose any time' by participating in this condition. Participation rates were virtually the same in the control condition and the regular viewing condition (54.2% vs 55.3%, respectively). Sufficient data were available for 93 subjects (48 control and 45 treated subjects). Statistical analyses were performed using SPSS/PC+ 4.0 software.

The two groups were not significantly different ($p = 0.05$) in terms of gender, age, pretest trait anxiety, pretest state anxiety, pretest concerns, posttest state anxiety, or posttest concerns, although the differences in pretest state anxiety fell just short of significance ($p = 0.051$). To assess the effects of the videotape on posttest state anxiety, an analysis of covariance using pretest state anxiety as the covariate was performed (Pedhazur & Schmelkin, 1991). Pretest state anxiety was the only significant predictor, accounting for 78% of the variance in posttest state anxiety. The intervention and the interaction of intervention and pretest state anxiety accounted for less than 1% of additional unique variance in posttest state anxiety. The same analysis for the other posttest variable of interest (specific concerns regarding hospitalization) used pretest concerns as the covariate. Similarly, specific patients' concerns at pretest accounted for slightly over 75% of the variance in specific concerns at posttest. The intervention and the interaction of intervention and pretest specific concerns accounted for less than 1% of additional unique variance in specific concerns at posttest.

This finding should be considered in light of the fact that 33 out of 45 experimental subjects indicated that they had not watched the video. Separate analysis of covariance for the two groups (experimental subjects who did and did not watch the video) again demonstrated that virtually all of the variance in posttest state anxiety and in posttest specific concerns was explained by their respective pretest scores.

Discussion

Although this was originally conceived as a randomized trial, subject self-selection into the study precludes inferences based on the assumption that randomization was achieved. There may have been differential selection into the experimental group by those initially higher in state anxiety and the change from pretest to posttest on state anxiety in the experimental group may have reflected regression towards the mean. Hypothesis guessing may also have occurred in both groups. These factors may have been operating because the institutional review board in the institution where the research was carried out required that subjects be given a full explanation of each of the experimental conditions in the informed consent. Generalization of these results is further restricted by the unique aspects of a patient sample from New York City.

Conclusions about the intervention are also affected by the fact that we found that 33 of 45 individuals in the experimental group did not watch the videotape. This might lead one to conclude that the treatment was not reliably implemented. We would disagree in that the point of this study was to evaluate the effects of a videotape intervention as it would likely be implemented in a busy admitting room. In reality, if admitting room staff tell incoming patients that a videotape is playing continuously for them, some individuals will choose to attend to it and some will not. We believe that this study did represent the treatment as it might be carried out in a nonexperimental setting.

The failure of the more structured viewing condition tells us that the priority for patients is getting through admissions as quickly as possible. Normally admissions requires that patients move from the waiting area to a number of offices and back again. If patients are asked if they are willing to move to yet another room, to engage in an activity that is presented as an optional aspect of admissions, it is easy to understand (in retrospect) the decision of many to decline to participate.

It is apparent that use of a videotape playing

TABLE I

COMPARISON OF PRE- AND POSTINTERVENTION DIFFERENCES BETWEEN CONTROL AND EXPERIMENTAL GROUPS ($N = 93$)

Variable	Control Group, $n = 48$		Experimental Group, $n = 45$	
	M	SD	M	SD
Gender (% women)	41.7		51.2	
Age (years)	51.1	16.6	53.1	15.6
Pretest Trait Anxiety	36.0	8.4	35.2	11.0
Pretest State Anxiety	41.0	13.8	46.7	13.8
Posttest State Anxiety	40.0	13.9	43.3	14.3
Pretest Specific concerns	2.2	.5	2.1	.6
Posttest Specific concerns	2.2	.6	2.1	.6

Note.—Higher scores on anxiety and concerns scales indicate higher anxiety or concern.

continuously in the admitting room was not supported in this study. Such use while perhaps helpful to some patients may in fact annoy others (e.g., readmissions who may have seen it previously, those waiting for admission for long time periods who might be exposed to the videotape multiple times, etc.). Yet there may be a group of individuals who might be interested in viewing such a videotape during admission. A potential solution that merits further study would be to allow individual viewing (e.g., with ear phones) of videotapes for those who desire to do so while experimentally varying the content of the videotape (e.g., male vs female or African-American vs Latin actors and actresses, amount of optimism portrayed, etc.). A videotape intervention may also be useful if employed at a different time. For instance, the patient might view the video prior to admission (e.g., in the office of the patient's private physician or in the patient's home) or once arriving in a hospital room (e.g., using a portable videotape setup on a cart or via closed circuit television). The use of informational media might also be extended to the preparation of current hospital patients for subsequent transitions to other institutions (e.g., nursing homes). Given the potential use of video tape for relatively low-cost improvement of patients' hospital experiences, these possibilities deserve further attention.

REFERENCES

ALLEN, K. D. DANFORTH, J. S. & DRABMAN, R. S. (1989) Videotaped modeling and film distraction for fear reduction in adults undergoing hyperbaric oxygen therapy. *Journal of Consulting and Clinical Psychology*, 57, 554–558.

GAGLIANO, M. E. (1988) A literature review on the efficacy of video in patient education. *Journal of Medical Education*, 63, 785–792.

KLEEMEIER, C. P., & HAZZARD, A. P. (1984) Videotaped parent education in pediatric waiting rooms. *Patient Education and Counseling*, 6, 122–124.

NIELSEN, E., & SHEPPARD, M. A. (1988) Television as a patient education tool: a review of its effectiveness. *Patient Education and Counseling*, 11, 3–16.

PEDHAZUR, E. J., & SCHMELKIN, L. P. (1991) *Measurement, design and analysis: an integrated approach.* Hillsdale, NJ: Erlbaum.

RASNAKE, L. K., & LINSCHEID, T. R. (1989) Anxiety reduction in children receiving medical care: developmental considerations. *Developmental and Behavioral Pediatrics*, 10, 169–175.

SPIELBERGER, C. D. (1983) *Manual for the State-Trait Anxiety Inventory.* Palo Alto, CA: Consulting Psychologists Press.

Accepted July 8, 1992

Step 3

After reading the Holden, Speedling, and Rosenberg (1992) study (Exhibit 12.3), answer the questions below.

1. How many total Quality Points did you give the Holden, Speedling, and Rosenberg article (1992) on the Quality of Study Rating Form? Please record Total Quality Points here:

   _____

2. What is its Effect Size 1 for Posttest State Anxiety? Please compute this and record your answer here:

   _____

3. Based on Total Quality Points and ES1, would you recommend that your hospital produce a short videotape to be shown to patients in admission?

   Yes _____   No _____

   Please explain the reasons for your answer:

   _____

   _____

   _____

   _____

   _____

   _____

FOLLOW-UP QUESTION

What have you learned by rating the Holden, Speedling, and Rosenberg article?

   _____

   _____

   _____

   _____

Exercise 13
DESCRIBING PROBLEMS: A KEY PART OF ASSESSMENT

PURPOSE

To demonstrate the importance of describing problems clearly.

BACKGROUND

This exercise demonstrates what happens when people base assessment on vague criteria. Assessment requires gathering and integrating information from a variety of sources. It provides a foundation for intervention (whether working with individuals, groups, or communities) and involves "looking before leaping" (defining problems clearly, discovering related factors, and deciding on outcomes).

Inaccurate assessment can waste time, effort, and resources; result in selecting ineffective or harmful plans; or cause miscommunication between clients and helpers or among different professionals. A key part of assessment is describing problems, such as depression and anxiety, clearly. In a vague assessment, descriptions of a problem are so fuzzy you don't really know what the problem is.

Efforts to clearly describe problems and discover related causes are subject to a variety of biases (e.g., seeing what you expect to see). Biases that get in the way of accurately describing problems are more likely to go unrecognized when problems are vaguely defined

Biases Related to Availability

Availability refers to the tendency to judge as most likely those events that can be readily imagined or recalled, perhaps because they are recent or vivid (Baron, 1994; Nisbett & Ross, 1980). One effect of availability on decision making is anchoring, or being influenced by initial impressions and not changing your opinion in light of new evidence (Tversky & Kahnerman, 1982). For example, when interviewers were told beforehand that the interviewee was either "extroverted" or "introverted," they asked questions that encouraged confirming data (Snyder & White, 1981). People tend to prejudge others based on race (Cousins, et al., 1986) and personal attractiveness (Johnson, et al., 1986; Nordholm, 1980). These characteristics are readily "available."

Bias Related to Representativeness

Representativeness refers to making decisions based on similarity. For example, people tend to believe that causes are similar to their effects. Stereotyping is a common example. People treat a description as if it represents all the individuals in a group, even when it does not.

INSTRUCTIONS

The videotape that accompanies this workbook includes a simulated interview with a client who may be "depressed." Your task is to apply four different definitions of depression to this client. Follow these steps as your instructor asks you to do them:

1. Read the following definition of depression. Underline each feature of depression described as you read it (do not compare notes or discuss your impressions while doing this).

   Depression. In psychiatry, a morbid state characterized by mood alterations, such as sadness and loneliness; by low self-esteem associated with self-reproach; by psychomotor retardation and at times agitation; by withdrawal from interpersonal contact and at times a desire to die; and by such vegetative symptoms as insomnia and anorexia. (Freedman, Kaplan, & Sadock, 1976)

2. Number each of the underlined features.
3. Repeat steps 1 and 2 for the following definition of depression.

   Depression is a term used to describe a mood, symptom, and syndromes of affective disorders. As a mood it refers to a transient state of feeling sad, blue, forlorn, cheerless, unhappy, and/or down. As a symptom, it refers to a complaint that often accompanies a group of biopsycho-social problems. In contrast, the depressive syndromes include a wide spectrum of psychobiological dysfunctions that vary in frequency, severity, and duration. Normal depression is a transient period of sadness and fatigue that generally occurs in response to identifiable stressful life events. The moods associated with normal depression vary in length but generally do not exceed 7 to 10 days. If the problems continue for a longer period and if the symptoms grow in complexity and severity, clinical levels of depression may be present. Clinical depression generally involves sleep disorders, eating disorders, anergia, hope-lessness, and despair. Sometimes problems assume psychotic proportions, and the depressed individual may attempt suicide and/or may experience hallucinations, delusions, and serious psychological and motor retardation. (Marsella, 1994)

4. Repeat steps 1 and 2 for the definition of depression in the Diagnostic and Statistical Manual for Mental Disorders–IV (DSM-IV) (American Psychiatric Association, 1994).

American Psychiatric Association's DSM-IV Definition of Depression: Criteria for Major Depressive Episode

A. Five (or more) of the following symptoms have been present during the same 2-week period and represent a change from previous functioning; at least one of the symptoms is either (1) depressed mood or (2) loss of interest or pleasure. *Note:* Do not include symptoms that are clearly due to a general medical condition, or mood-incongruent delusions or hallucinations.

   (1) depressed mood most of the day, nearly every day, as indicated by either subjective report (e.g., feels sad or empty) or observation made by others (e.g., appears tearful). *Note:* In children and adolescents, can be irritable mood.

   (2) markedly diminished interest or pleasure in all, or almost all, activities most of the day, nearly every day (as indicated by either subjective account or observation made by others).

   (3) significant weight loss when not dieting or weight gain (e.g., a change of more than 5% of body weight in a month), or decrease or increase in appetite nearly every day. *Note:* In children, consider failure to make expected weight gains.

   (4) insomnia or hypersomnia nearly every day.

   (5) psychomotor agitation or retardation nearly every day (observable by others, not merely subjective feelings of restlessness or being slowed down).

   (6) fatigue or loss of energy nearly every day.

   (7) feelings of worthlessness or excessive or inappropriate guilt (which may be delusional) nearly every day (not merely self-reproach or guilt about being sick).

   (8) diminished ability to think or concentrate, or indecisiveness, nearly every day (either by subjective account or as observed by others).

   (9) recurrent thoughts of death (not just fear of dying), recurrent suicidal ideation without a specific plan, or a suicide attempt or a specific plan for committing suicide.

B. The symptoms do not meet criteria for a mixed episode.

C. The symptoms cause clinically significant distress or impairment in social, occupational, or other important areas of functioning.

D. The symptoms are not due to the direct physiological effects of a substance (e.g., a drug of abuse, a medication) or a general medical condition (e.g., hypothyroidism).

E. The symptoms are not better accounted for by bereavement, i.e., after the loss of a loved one, the symptoms persist for longer than 2 months or are characterized by marked functional impairment, morbid preoccupation with worthlessness, suicidal ideation, psychotic symptoms, or psychomotor retardation (American Psychiatric Association, 1994).

5. When everyone has completed steps 1–4, your instructor will show Part D of the videotape. While you watch it, record here all indicators of depression that you observe.

_____

_____

_____

_____

_____

_____

_____

_____

_____

_____

_____

_____

_____

_____

_____

_____

_____

_____

_____

_____

_____

_____

_____

_____

_____

_____

6. Refer back to the Freedman, Kaplan, and Sadock (1976) definition of depression. How many features of depression from this definition did you see demonstrated in the interview? Insert the number here:

_____

Compute the following:

$$\left(\frac{\text{Number of features of depression from Freedman, Kaplan, and Sadock definition (1976) seen in the interview}}{\text{Total number of features of depression in Freedman, Kaplan, and Sadock (1976) written definition}} \right) \times 100$$

= _____ %

7. Compute this same percentage for the Marsella (1994) definition:

_____ %

8. Compute this same percentage for the DSM-IV definition:

_____ %

9. Next, note the client's responses on the Zung Depression Scale (see Exhibit 13.1).

Exhibit 13.1   **THE ZUNG SELF-RATING DEPRESSION SCALE (SDS)**

Items	A A Little of the Time	B Some of the time	C Good Part of the Time	D Most of the Time	Item Weights* A	B	C	D
1. I feel down-hearted and blue		✓			1	2	3	4
2. Morning is when I feel the best			✓		4	3	2	1
3. I have crying spells or feel like crying	✓				1	2	3	4
4. I have trouble sleeping at night		✓			1	2	3	4
5. I eat as much as I used to			✓		4	3	2	1
6. I still enjoy sex			✓		4	3	2	1
7. I notice that I am losing weight	✓				1	2	3	4
8. I have trouble with constipation		✓			1	2	3	4
9. My heart beats faster than usual		✓			1	2	3	4
10. I get tired for no reason			✓		1	2	3	4
11. My mind is as clear as it used to be		✓			4	3	2	1
12. I find it easy to do the things I used to		✓			4	3	2	1
13. I am restless and can't keep still		✓			1	2	3	4
14. I feel hopeful about the future	✓				4	3	2	1
15. I am more irritable than usual		✓			1	2	3	4
16. I find it easy to make decisions			✓		4	3	2	1
17. I feel that I am useful and needed		✓			4	3	2	1
18. My life is pretty full	✓				4	3	2	1
19. I feel that others would be better off if I were dead		✓			1	2	3	4
20. I still enjoy the things I used to do		✓			4	3	2	1

*Item weights should not appear on actual measure.

Instructions for Administration: Tell the client, "I am going to ask you to answer a series of 20 questions according to how you feel right now. Please answer each question according to the one response that best applies to you, "A Little of the Time, Some of the Time, Good Part of the Time, Most of the Time." (Then read each question and record the client's answer. If the client asks you to clarify the question, reread the question and ask that the client answer it according to the item's meaning or how they interpret it.

Instructions for Scoring: Sum the weights for the client's response to all 20 items. Compute the subject's score by dividing the subject's score by 80 and multiplying by 100 to get a percent. For example, for a score of 56, this would be the score (56/80)100 = 70%.
An explanation of how to interpret this score goes beyond space available here, but generally, the higher the value the more depressed the client.

10. Compute the total score on the client's Zung Scale by adding the response weights (1, 2, 3, or 4) for each of the twenty items.

Score = _____

11. Compute a percentage as follows:

$$\frac{\text{Total on the Zung}}{80} \times 100 =$$

_____ %

12. You now have four numbers representing your rating of the client's level of depression using four different criteria. The first three definitions (Freedman, et al., 1976; Marsella, 1994; DSM-IV, 1994) are conceptual definitions. They use abstract conceptual words and phrases to describe what to look for. The fourth definition is based on a standardized measure (the Zung Depression Inventory). You can derive a score that allows you to compare clients or a single client at different times (before and after counseling). Standardized measures are accompanied by a description of how to score and interpret responses. Keep in mind, however, that just because a measure is standardized, it is not necessarily valid. That is, it may not measure what it is designed to measure (see later discussion on reliability and validity).

13. Your instructor will ask each class member to read his or her percent value for each definition. As the values are read, plot them on the appropriate bar below with a heavy circle on the bar for each student's value. If more than one student gives the same value, stack the circles above the first over the appropriate value on the bar.

Freedman, Kaplan, and Sadock (1976)

0 10 20 30 40 50 60 70 80 90 100

Mean = _____

SD = _____

Marsella (1994)

0 10 20 30 40 50 60 70 80 90 100

Mean = _____

SD = _____

DSM-IV (1994)

0 10 20 30 40 50 60 70 80 90 100

Mean = _____

SD = _____

Zung (1975)

0 10 20 30 40 50 60 70 80 90 100

Mean = _____

SD = _____

1. Of the four definitions, which one yielded the most agreement among class members about the level of the client's depression (i.e., which is most reliable)?

   _____

2. Do you think this client is experiencing emotional pain?

   Yes _____ No _____ Discuss your reasons.

   _____

   _____

   _____

   _____

   _____

3. Could this problem be life threatening?

   Yes _____ No _____ Discuss your reasons.

   _____

   _____

   _____

   _____

   _____

4. What do the results imply for other clients? Labels are used to categorize people (e.g., alcoholic, hyperactive, sexually abused, autistic, sexually dysfunctional). Hundreds of diagnostic labels are included in the DSM-IV (American Psychiatric Association, 1994). Interventions may be selected on the basis of problem definitions. What does this exercise imply for this client as well as others?

   _____

   _____

   _____

   _____

   _____

   _____

   _____

   _____

5. What does this exercise imply for practitioners?

_____

_____

_____

_____

_____

_____

_____

6. How does this exercise illustrate the difference between diagnosis and assessment?

_____

_____

_____

_____

_____

_____

_____

7. Are reliable measures valid? A measure is *reliable* when different observers arrive at very similar ratings using that measure; it is *valid* when it measures what it is designed to measure. Assuming that standardized measures are valid would be a mistake.

_____

_____

_____

_____

_____

_____

_____

_____

Question 7 raises a vital concern about the relationship between reliability and validity in measurement. Because this question may assume more background than some readers have, the section below outlines some concepts.

Reliability refers to the consistency of results provided by the same person at different times (time-based reliability), by two different raters of the same events (individual-based reliability, as in inter-rater reliability), or by parallel forms or split-halfs of a measure (item-bound reliability). The first kind is known as test-retest reliability. If a measure is not reliable, you cannot find out if it is valid. For example, if responses on a questionnaire vary from time to time in the absence of real change, you cannot use it to predict what a person will do in the future. Reliability can be assessed in a number of ways, all of which yield some measure of consistency.

In *test-retest reliability,* the scores of the same individuals at different times are correlated with each other. We might administer the Zung to several persons whom we think might be "depressed," then administer it again with the same instructions a few days or weeks later to see if the scores are similar over time. Correlations may range from +1 to −1. The size of the correlation coefficient indicates the degree of association. A zero correlation indicates a complete absence of consistency. A correlation of +1 indicates a perfect correlation. The stability (reliability of a measure at different times) of some measures is high. That is, you can ask a client to complete a questionnaire this week and five weeks from now and obtain similar results (in the absence of real change). Other measures have low stability. Coefficients of reliability are usually sufficient if they are .70 or better. However, the higher the better. What do you know about the test-retest reliability of the Zung?

Homogeneity is a measure of internal consistency. It assesses the degree to which all the items on a test measure the same characteristics. The homogeneity of a test (as measured, for example, by "coefficient alpha") is important if all the items on it are supposed to measure the same characteristics. If a scale is multidimensional (e.g., many dimensions are assumed to be involved in a construct such as "loneliness" or "social support"), then homogeneity among all items would not be expected. The Zung's *internal consistency* might be evaluated by computing the correlations of all twenty items with the Zung's total score and averaging these correlations. We could compute Zung's *split-half reliability* by dividing the Zung's items randomly into two groups of ten items each, administering both halves to a group of subjects, then seeing if the halves correlate well with each other.

Validity concerns the question, Does the measure reflect the characteristics it is supposed to measure? For example, does a client's behavior in a role play correspond to what the client does in similar real-life situations? Direct measures are typically more valid than indirect measures. For instance, observing teacher-student interaction will probably offer more accurate data than asking a student to complete a questionnaire assumed to offer information about classroom behavior.

There are many kinds of validity.

Predictive validity refers to the extent to which a measure accurately predicts behavior at a later time. For example, how accurately does a measure of suicidal potential predict suicide attempts? Can you accurately predict what a person will do in the future from his or her score on the Zung?

Concurrent validity refers to the extent to which a measure correlates with a validated measure gathered at the same time; for example, do responses on a questionnaire concerning social behavior correspond to behavior in real-life settings? Do scores on the Zung correlate with other well-accepted criterion measures of depression in predicted ways?

Criterion validity is used to refer to predictive and concurrent validity.

Content validity reflects the degree to which a measure adequately samples the domain being assessed. For example, does an inventory used to assess parenting skills include an adequate sample of such skills? Do items on the Zung adequately represent the domain of interest (depression)?

Face validity refers to the extent to which items included on a measure make sense "on the face of it." Given the intent of the instrument, would you expect the included items to be there? Can you tell what the questions are designed to "tap" on the Zung?

Construct validity refers to the degree to which a measure successfully measures a theoretical construct—the degree to which results of a measure correspond to assumptions about the measure. The finding that depressed people report more negative thoughts on the Automatic Thoughts Questionnaire (Hollon & Kendall, 1980) compared with nondepressed people adds an increment of construct validity to this measure. In a measure that has construct validity, different methods of assessing a construct (e.g., direct observation and self-report) yield similar results, and similar methods of measuring *different* constructs (e.g., aggression and altruism) yield different results. That is, evidence should be available that a construct can be distinguished from different constructs. For a description of different ways construct validity can be established, see for example, Anastasi (1989). Do scores on the Zung correlate in predicted ways with other measures? They should have a positive correlation with other measures of depression and a negative correlation with measures of happiness, good cheer, and glee, for example.

Exercise 14
MAKING PREDICTIONS

Your Name _____ Date _____

Course _____

Instructor's Name _____

PURPOSE

1. To introduce you to some concepts basic to risk assessment and decision making, such as sensitivity, specificity, positive predictive value, and base rate.
2. To increase your awareness of key elements in assessing risk.
3. To encourage you to read further about decision analysis.

BACKGROUND

Risk assessment and making decisions based on assessed risk are integral to helping clients. Decisions made by physicians and nurses can affect their clients' survival. Mental-health workers assess the risk of harm to clients (suicide) and others (homicide). Child-welfare workers make judgments about the potential risk of child abuse. Teachers screen children for learning and interpersonal problems and refer children for intervention. Risk assessment is universal to all the helping professions.

Helpers usually base decisions about their clients on their *implicit* estimation of the likelihood of certain events. They usually do not describe estimates in terms of specific probabilities, but will often describe their judgments in such words as *probably, most likely, surely, possibly, certainly, somewhat likely, maybe,* or *high risk.*

This exercise asks you to estimate the likelihood of events in terms of *explicit* (specific) probabilities, from 0% (certain not to happen), to 50% (as likely to happen as not), to 100% (certain to happen). Let's say that you are asked to estimate the likelihood that we will all die someday. You might say that this event is "certain" (100% probability). If a doctor is asked, "What is the probability that an eighty-year-old white male patient will die within the next five years?" he might say, "Very likely" and translate this estimation to a 44% probability based on a life expectancy table (Sox, Blatt, Higgins, & Marton, 1988). A member of a parole board might be asked about the likelihood that a given inmate will be charged for and be convicted of another criminal offense within the first eighteen months after the inmate's release from prison. If pressed to be explicit, the parole board member might say that the chance of this is "fairly low," meaning 20%.

People make judgments and decisions based on both prior and new information. For example, you may have prior information about clients before you see them. When you interview clients, you gather new information. A parole board member in Nevada may know that 30 of the last 100 inmates released from prison committed a new offense within eighteen months of their release. Knowing this, and nothing more about an inmate about to be released, the parole-board member would have to estimate that there is a 30% chance (prior probability) that the inmate will commit more crimes. To increase accuracy, the parole-board member may gather additional information about the client by completing a risk-assessment scale based on the inmate's prior history.

This exercise introduces Bayes's Theorem as a way to integrate prior and new information about a client's history to help you judge the likelihood of his or her behavior. Bayes's Theorem is a major tool in an emerging science of clinical decision-analysis (Elstein, Dawson-Saunders, & Belzer, 1985; Gibbs, 1994; Sox, et al., 1988; Weinstein, Fineberg, Elstein, Frazier, Neuhauser, Neutra, & McNeil, 1980).

INSTRUCTIONS

Follow the next four steps.

Step 1

Read the description of each situation that follows and give the requested probability estimates. We will give you information about the following:

1. *Prior probability*—the likelihood that the client has a particular problem, given only the information that you have *before* you do your assessment work
2. *Sensitivity*—among those known to have a problem, the proportion whom a test or measure said had the problem
3. *Specificity*—among those known not to have the problem, the proportion whom the test or measure has said did not have the problem

Based on the prior probability, sensitivity, and specificity given in Situations 1–4 below, estimate the probability requested and record your answer.

SITUATION 1   *Imagine that you are an administrator in a community correction agency that serves criminal offender clients on probation.* From agency records you know that 3% of your clients committed a new offense during the past year and were sent to prison. Thus, 3% is the prior probability, and your best estimate, that a new client who is referred to your agency will commit further crimes in the next year, knowing nothing more about a client.

Now, let's say that you have a new assessment tool called the Probation Risk Assessment Measure (PRAM). PRAM's sensitivity is 95%, that is, you know from experience with the measure last year that 95% of those who failed on probation had tested positively—the test had said they would fail. PRAM's specificity is 93%, that is, you know from experience with the measure last year that 93% of those who had tested negatively— the test had said they would not fail—did not commit more crimes. Given these three values—3% prior probability, 95% sensitivity, and 93% specificity—and that PRAM indicates that client X will commit further crimes within the next year, what is your estimate that the client will?

Your estimate: _____

Estimate based on Bayes's Theorem
(calculate this later): _____

SITUATION 2   *Imagine again that you are an administrator in a community correction agency that serves criminal offender clients on parole (conditional release from a prison).* From agency records you know that 35% of your clients committed a new offense during the past year and were sent to prison. Thus, 35% is the prior probability (and your best estimate) that a new client whom you know nothing else about will commit further crimes in the next year.

Imagine you have used the Probation Risk Assessment Measure (PRAM), which has a sensitivity of 95% and a specificity of 93%. Given these three values—35% prior probability, 95% sensitivity, and 93% specificity—and that PRAM indicates that client X will recidivate within the next year, what is your estimate that the client will?

Your estimate: _____

Estimate based on Bayes's Theorem
(calculate this later): _____

SITUATION 3   *You are an administrator who heads the Medically Fragile Special-Education Needs Program in Midwestern School District.* Your agency receives 300 referrals from teachers, parents, and physicians each year, which must be evaluated to see which children in the district should get special services. Your records show that, during the past year, 50% of those referred needed services, according to a three-hour Battelle Developmental Inventory followed by interviews and a multidisciplinary team evaluation.

You are thinking of using the Denver Developmental Screening Test (DST), which takes less time to complete. This has a sensitivity of 94% (i.e., you know from experience that 94% of those who were said to need services by the DST did need services) and a specificity of 97% (i.e., you know from experience that 97% of those indicated as not needing services did not need services). What is the probability that clients referred this year who are tested with DST and found by DST to need services in fact will need services?

Your estimate: _____

Estimate based on Bayes's Theorem
(calculate this later): _____

SITUATION 4   *Again, you are an administrator who heads the Medically Fragile Special-Education Needs Program in Midwestern School District.* You are considering administering a Denver Developmental Screening Test (DST) to all preschool and grade-school children in your district to determine which children should receive your agency's services. Your records show that during the past year, 150 (1%) of 15,000 children in your school district needed services. The DST has a 94% sensitivity and a 97% specificity.

If 15,000 children are screened with DST, what is the probability that they will in fact need services if the DST indicated they do?

Your estimate: _____

Estimate based on Bayes's Theorem
(calculate this later): _____

Step 2

Insert the values for prevalence rate, sensitivity, and specificity in the formula for Bayes's Theorem (given here) to find the predictive value of a positive test result for Situation 1.

BAYES'S THEOREM $$PPV = \frac{(\text{Prevalence})(\text{Sensitivity})}{(\text{Prevalence})(\text{Sensitivity}) + (1 - \text{Prevalence})(1 - \text{Specificity})}$$

Step 3

Compare your answer with the one below. We have worked out Bayes's Theorem for Situation 1 to provide a model for solving Situations 2–4.

$$PPV = \frac{(.03)(.95)}{(.03)(.95) + (1 - .03)(1 - .93)} = .30 \text{ or } 30\%$$

Step 4

Compute the predictive value of a positive test for Situations 2–4 and record your answers next to your estimates in Situations 1–4.

FOLLOW-UP QUESTIONS

1. Do you think that social workers accurately use prevalence rate, sensitivity, and specificity to arrive at an accurate estimate of the predictive value of a positive test result?

    Yes _____   No _____

    Please give reasons for your answer:

    _____

    _____

    _____

    _____

2. Is the predictive value of a positive test greater where the prevalence rate is relatively high? (*Hint:* Compare Situation 1 with Situation 2, Situation 3 with Situation 4.)

    _____

    _____

    _____

    _____

3. Compare all four values of your estimated probabilities with those computed with Bayes's Theorem. Did you tend to overestimate or underestimate probabilities compared with those found by using Bayes's Theorem?

    _____

    _____

    _____

    _____

    _____

    _____

    _____

    _____

Exercise 15
CRITICAL THINKING AS A GUIDE TO MAKING ETHICAL DECISIONS

PURPOSE

To illustrate the value of critical thinking as a guide to making ethical decisions in professional helping contexts.

BACKGROUND

Some think the very purpose of critical thinking is to arrive at moral or ethical decisions (Baron, 1985). Barbara Thayer-Bacon (1993) says,

> Most critical thinking theories address the problems of how to develop reasoning abilities and to encourage students to be more rational. I would like to argue that there is another necessary quality for being a critical thinker that is as important as the propensity to be rational: The ability to be receptive, caring, and open to others' ideas and willing to attend to them, to listen and consider their possibilities. . . . Caring is necessary to be sure ideas have been fairly considered and understood. (p. 323)

Ethical dilemmas (e.g., situations in which there are competing interests) require careful consideration from all points of view to be resolved in the best possible way.

INSTRUCTIONS

1. Review the Checklist of Ethical Concerns in Exhibit 15.1.
2. Select vignettes in Games A, B, and/or C to review. Your instructor may help you choose them.
3. Note the game and vignette number and ethical issue that you think is evident in that vignette on the form in Exhibit 15.2. Note any other issues that you think apply.

Exhibit 15.1　**CHECKLIST OF ETHICAL CONCERNS**

A. *Keeping Confidentiality*

____ 1. Limits on confidentiality are described.

____ 2. Confidentiality is maintained unless there are concerns about harm to others.

B. *Selecting Objectives*

____ 3. Objectives focused on result in real-life gains for clients.

____ 4. Objectives are related to the key concerns of clients.

C. *Selecting Methods*

____ 5. Assessment methods relied on are likely to provide accurate, relevant information.

____ 6. Intervention methods selected are likely to attain outcomes that clients value.

____ 7. Assessment, intervention, and evaluation methods are acceptable to clients.

D. *Fully Informing Clients*

____ 8. Clients are given an accurate description of the accuracy of assessment methods used.

____ 9. Clients receive accurate estimates of the likely success of recommended procedures.

____10. Alternative methods and their likely success are described.

____11. Clear descriptions of the cost, time, and effort involved in a suggested method are presented in language intelligible to clients.

____12. An accurate description and the likelihood of side effects (both positive and negative) of suggested services is provided.

____13. An accurate description of the helper's competence to offer needed services is provided.

____14. Appropriate arrangements are made to involve others in decisions when clients cannot give informed consent.

E. *Being Competent*

____15. Helpers are competent to use the assessment measures they rely on.

____16. Helpers are competent to use the intervention methods they rely on.

F. *Being Accountable*

____17. Arrangements are made for ongoing feedback about progress using valid progress indicators.

G. *Encouraging a Culture of Thoughtfulness*

____18. Positive feedback is provided to colleagues for the critical evaluation of claims and arguments.

____19. Efforts are made to change agency procedures and policies that interfere with service.

Exhibit 15.2   **VIGNETTES REVIEWED FOR ETHICAL CONCERNS**

Your Name _____   Date _____

Course _____

Instructor's Name _____

REASONING-IN-PRACTICE VIGNETTES	*Game*	*Number*	*Ethical Issue*
	_____	_____	_____
	_____	_____	_____
	_____	_____	_____
	_____	_____	_____
	_____	_____	_____
	_____	_____	_____
	_____	_____	_____
	_____	_____	_____
	_____	_____	_____
	_____	_____	_____
	_____	_____	_____
	_____	_____	_____
	_____	_____	_____
	_____	_____	_____

Exhibit 15.2 (continued)	Game	Number	Ethical Issue
	_____	_____	_____
	_____	_____	_____
	_____	_____	_____
	_____	_____	_____
	_____	_____	_____
	_____	_____	_____
	_____	_____	_____
	_____	_____	_____
	_____	_____	_____

FOLLOW-UP QUESTIONS

1. Do you feel ethically bound to think critically about your practice? Why or why not?

_____

_____

_____

_____

_____

2. Please identify any particular game, vignette, or ethical issue that you think particularly important.

_____

_____

_____

_____

_____

Exercise 16
ERROR AS PROCESS: TEMPLATING, JUSTIFICATION, AND RATCHETING

PURPOSE

This exercise introduces three sources of error highlighted by Howitt (1992) that may result in faulty decisions: templating, justification, and ratcheting. Each is explained and an opportunity is provided to practice identifying them.

BACKGROUND

Templating involves checking the individual against a "social template" to see whether or not he or she fits a particular pattern. An instigating event, such as a bruise or scratch detected on a child by a health visitor, leads to the "suspect" person being compared with the template. Howitt (1992) believes that templating differs from stereotyping because the latter involves attributing characteristics to individuals not because of a specific event, but because they belong to a broad category of people (e.g., she is a "bad driver" because she is a "woman," not because she has gotten into three accidents in the last month). Such stereotyping is often obvious and likely to be rejected.

Justification refers to using theory to "justify" decisions rather than critically examining the beliefs and evidence that have influenced the decisions. For example, some child protection errors result from theoretical points of view that justify contradictory courses of action. A classic example is the "contrition belief," or the assumption that a family or family member is only "treatable" if they understand the implications of and admit responsibility for what has happened. If they say they did abuse the child, the child is removed; if they say they did not, they are assumed to be lying, and the child is removed. Thus, for the family in which abuse has *not* occurred, a truthful denial is no different in its outcome from false denial in families with abuse. The family is damned if it does and damned if it doesn't. The theory justifies all possible explanations and increases the risk that a child will be or remain separated from his or her family. Focusing on justification rather than on critically examining your beliefs may result in errors based on "pseudodiagnosticity," where some assumption that may be true in relation to some cases is overgeneralized to many cases.

Ratcheting refers to a tendency for the child-protection processes to move in a single direction. Changing a decision or undoing its effects seems infrequent, even in circumstances where these are appropriate. Consider the difference between *taking-into-care* and *coming-out-of-care* decisions. Criteria governing the former may differ from those of the latter. A troublesome child may enter care to provide respite for his or her parents. However, when the parents feel able to cope, child-protection workers may not return the child home. Ratcheting has a "never going back" quality that may appear to protect the helper by reducing the chances of a "risky" decision resulting in problems and criticism.

INSTRUCTIONS

1. Read the Background information above.
2. Read the Case Example (Exhibit 16.1).
3. Write your answers to the questions in "Error As Process" (Exhibit 16.2).
4. Discuss your answers with your instructor and other students.

Exhibit 16.1   **CASE EXAMPLE FOR EXERCISE 16**

The key events began shortly after the family had moved into a new home. The family consisted of Mr. and Mrs. Fletcher and Stuart (age three), who was from a previous relationship of Mrs. Fletcher's. Mrs. Fletcher was twenty-seven and the husband was thirty years old. The couple were married about five weeks before the precipitating incident took place. Stuart was in bed, and it was about 10:30 P.M. According to his mother, he got up to go to the toilet. Climbing over a safety gate at the top of the stairs, he caught his foot in it and fell down the steps. Alerted by his call, the parents picked him up. They found a carpet burn on the side of his knee. However, the next morning he complained of a "headache." Concerned about the possibility of a concussion, Mrs. Fletcher examined him further but could find additionally only "two tiny little bruises on his rib cage." She telephoned her doctor, who suggested that she should visit his surgery. Coincidentally, the health visitor arrived (Mrs. Fletcher was pregnant) and drove them there. Mrs. Fletcher described what happened.

> So we got there and he examined Stuart. . . . He said to Stuart how have you done this? And Stuart said I fell down the stairs last night because I climbed over the safety gate and I was naughty, you know . . . and then the doctor said to him has your mummy hit you? And Stuart said no. And he said has your daddy hit you? And Stuart said no . . . and he said I'm very sorry to say this but I think either you or your husband has abused your son, in other words you've hit him: what have you got to say? And I said well that's just ridiculous. I mean this was my family doctor, who'd known me since I was born myself.

Her doctor asked her to take Stuart to see a hospital pediatrician, whose views were that "this is just a waste of time" since the injuries and the story were perfectly consistent and that "there is no evidence in my opinion that this child has been abused at all." Mrs. Fletcher was told to go home,

> at which point there was a knock at the door and a nurse said could she have a word with the pediatrician. . . . So he went out, he was gone for 5 minutes, and he came back in. And he said I'm very sorry Mrs. Fletcher, but your doctor has rung the social services and informed them that he thinks that the child is at risk, and a social worker was there at the hospital. . . . In the

---

*Adapted from Dennis Howitt, *Child Abuse Errors,* copyright © 1992 by Dennis Howitt. Reprinted by permission of Rutgers University Press.

space of two hours, this was, social services have been to a magistrate and they've taken a place of safety order, just on the say-so of my doctor.

In the meantime, the police arrived at the hospital. Mrs. Fletcher's parents also got there after being telephoned. Eventually her husband also reached the hospital. He was immediately arrested by two police officers in spite of the fact that the idea that he abused Stuart was ridiculous—Stuart had fallen down the stairs.

> They said your wife doesn't want anything to do with you so you might as well tell us the truth, because she knows you've been hitting your son and she's just totally disgusted with you, in fact you're probably never going to see her again . . .

> . . . this policeman sat by him and gave him a cigarette, and he said I can't say as I blame you because after all he's not yours is he. Somebody's been with your wife before you, how does that make you feel? I bet you hate that child. The husband said well he's not mine but, you know, I think of him as my son.

The father was not prosecuted. Within a few days, Mrs. Fletcher miscarried and she attributes this to the child-abuse allegations. She claims no prior or later miscarriages. Within four weeks of the intervention, a court application for an interim-care order failed because of a lack of evidence, but a two-week adjournment was granted. In the end, no substantial evidence was provided.

> All they said was we've visited Mr. and Mrs. Fletcher in their home and we feel because the father is not the natural father, we believe that he, the son, is at risk from the stepfather, because he isn't the natural father. . . . They're a new family, they've only just been married, they've only just moved into this house, and we feel that the son is at risk and should remain on the at risk register . . . and that they should have this care order.

Eventually, the boy's name was removed from the at-risk register. This Mrs. Fletcher saw as being the consequence of the threat of a judicial review of the case. All through the period of being on the at-risk register, Mr. Fletcher's children from a previous marriage had visited for overnight stays. After the removal from the at-risk register,

> my husband's ex-wife was contacted by the social services where she lives. . . . She had this note saying would she please telephone this particular social worker . . . So she went alone and the social worker told her that her ex-husband had been accused of child abuse, and that in his opinion he didn't think that the children should be allowed to come down here and see their father unless it was in the presence of their grandmother, like my husband's mother.

Exhibit 16.2   **ERROR AS PROCESS**

Your Name   Date

Course

Instructor's Name

Give an example of each source of error from the case example.

1. Templating:

_____

_____

_____

_____

2. Justification:

_____

_____

_____

_____

3. Ratcheting:

_____

_____

_____

_____

1. How do your answers compare with those of other students?

_____

_____

_____

_____

_____

_____

_____

2. Have you observed any of these three dysfunctional patterns of thinking? If so, please describe what you observed and the consequences of such thinking.

_____

_____

_____

_____

_____

_____

_____

_____

_____

_____

_____

_____

_____

_____

_____

_____

_____

_____

_____

_____

Exercise 17
EVALUATING DIAGNOSTIC TESTS

Your Name _____   Date _____

Course _____

Instructor's Name _____

PURPOSE

To enhance skills in selecting assessment measures and highlight the dangers of using tests that do not measure what they claim to measure.

BACKGROUND

Professionals often use tests to make decisions about clients. These tests may either provide helpful guidelines or offer misleading data that appear to inform but do the opposite—harm rather than help clients. Consider the example of the reflex dilation test. In Britain, Hobbs and Wynne (1986) (two pediatricians) suggested that a simple medical test could be used to demonstrate that buggery or other forms of anal penetration had occurred. Here is their description:

> Reflex dilation, well described in forensic texts . . . usually occurs within about 30 seconds of separating the buttocks. Recent controversy has helped our understanding of what is now seen as an important sign of traumatic penetration of the anus as occurs in abuse, but also following medical and surgical manipulation. . . . The diameter of the symmetrical relaxation of the anal sphincter is variable and should be estimated. This is a dramatic sign which once seen is easily recognized. . . . The sign is not always easily reproducible on second and third examinations and there appear to be factors, at present, which may modify the eliciting of this physical sign. The sign in most cases gradually disappears when abuse stops. (Hanks, Hobbs, & Wynne, 1988, p. 153)

News of this test spread quickly, and because of this test many children were removed from their homes on the grounds that they were being sexually abused.

QUESTIONS

1. What questions should be raised about the reflex dilation test? Please list each separately and describe why you would ask this question. You may find it helpful to review material on reliability and validity in Exercise 13 as well as discussion of false positive and false negative rates in Exercise 14.

_____

_____

_____

_____

_____

_____

_____

2. Would you use this test?

Yes _____   No _____

Please explain your answer:

_____

_____

_____

_____

_____

_____

_____

_____

_____

_____

_____

_____

Exercise 18
REVIEWING INTERVENTION PLANS

PURPOSE

To enhance skills in reviewing intervention plans.

BACKGROUND

Professionals make decisions about what service plans may prevent or remove problems. The checklist included in this exercise describes points to check when deciding on plans. For example will there be any negative side effects, are cultural differences considered, are plans acceptable to clients and significant others, and does practice-related research suggest that plans selected will be effective? It is easy to forget about the many dimensions of service plans that should be considered.

INSTRUCTIONS

1. Select a client with whom you have decided on, or are deciding on, service plans (or your instructor may provide a case example).
2. Apply the Checklist for Reviewing Intervention Plans (Exhibit 18.1) to the material provided.
3. Add up the circled numbers to determine an overall score. Total score can range from 0 to 66.

Score = _____

Exhibit 18.1   **CHECKLIST FOR REVIEWING INTERVENTION PLANS**

Your Name   Date

Course

Instructor's Name

N = Not at all satisfactory   **L** = A little satisfactory   **S** = Satisfactory   **I** = Ideal

No.	Item	N	L	S	I
1.	Assessment data support the plan's selection.	0	1	2	3
2.	The plan addresses problem-related circumstances.	0	1	2	3
3.	The plan is feasible.	0	1	2	3
4.	The plan and rationales for it are acceptable to participants.	0	1	2	3
5.	The plan, including intermediate steps, is clearly described.	0	1	2	3
6.	The plan relies on positive methods.	0	1	2	3
7.	The plan allows for the incremental acquisition of skills in accord with available skills.	0	1	2	3
8.	The plan is not overly intrusive.	0	1	2	3
9.	The plan is efficient in cost, time, and effort.	0	1	2	3
10.	The plan selected offers the greatest likelihood of success.*	0	1	2	3
11.	Positive side effects are likely.	0	1	2	3
12.	Negative side effects are unlikely.	0	1	2	3
13.	Significant others are involved.	0	1	2	3
14.	Cues and reinforcers for desired behaviors are arranged.	0	1	2	3
15.	Cues and reinforcers for undesired behaviors are removed.	0	1	2	3
16.	The plan arranges for generalization and maintenance of valued outcomes.	0	1	2	3
17.	Chosen settings maximize the likelihood of success.	0	1	2	3
18.	Cultural differences are considered.	0	1	2	3
19.	Multiple services are well integrated.	0	1	2	3
20.	Participants are given a written description of the plan.	0	1	2	3
21.	The plan meets legal and ethical requirements.	0	1	2	3
22.	The probability that the plan will be successful in removing complaints is high ($p > .80$).	0	1	2	3

*Standards to review when answering item 10:
- There is scientific evidence that your plan will be effective with this problem.
- There are empirically based principles that suggest that your plan will be effective with this client.
- There is scientific evidence that this plan is likely to be more effective than other plans.

1. Is there any way you could increase the likelihood of success given available resources?

Yes _____   No _____

If *No,* this is because

_____ I have selected the plan most likely to be successful. (Describe criteria you used to make this selection.)

_____ I don't know how to offer other plans that have been found to be more likely to succeed.

_____ I know how to offer more effective services but don't have the time. (How much more time would you need?)

_____ I don't have access to the resources needed to offer a more effective plan. (Clearly describe what you need).

_____ The client is not willing to participate.

_____ Other (please describe).

Please explain your answer, if directed to do so, here:

_____

_____

_____

If *Yes,* please explain how:

_____

_____

_____

_____

2. Are there any items on the checklist that you do not think are important? If so, why?

_____

_____

_____

3. What items do you think are especially important from the client's point of view?

_____

_____

_____

_____

Exercise 19
ANALYZING ARGUMENTS

PURPOSE

To increase skill in analyzing arguments.

BACKGROUND

Argument analysis is a vital practice skill. Practitioners hear and offer arguments daily for and against life-affecting decisions. Here, we define an argument not as a conflict, but as a group of statements, one or more of which (the premises) are assumed to provide evidence for another (the conclusion). An argument is used to suggest the truth or demonstrate the falsity of a particular claim. A key part of an argument is the claim, conclusion, or position put forward. (Excessive wordiness may make a conclusion difficult to identify.) A second is reasons or premises offered to support the claim. These reasons will differ in their relevance to a claim, in their acceptability, and in their sufficiency to support a claim. (See the section describing guidelines for evaluating arguments on pp. 206–208.) A third component of arguments consists of the reasons given for assuming that the premises are relevant to the conclusion. These are called warrants.

Let's say a teacher consults the school psychologist about Willie, who is a a hard-to-manage student. The psychologist tells the teacher that the student is hyperactive and should be placed on Ritalin because it has been found to decrease hyperactivity. What is her premise? What warrants are appealed to? Are there alternative accounts (rival hypotheses) that point to a different conclusion? Can an analogy be used to support an opposing conclusion? (For practice in identifying rival hypotheses, see Huck & Sandler, 1979). Some conclusions can be supported by good reasons, others have weak support. "A good argument . . . offers reasons and evidence so that other people can make up their minds for themselves" (Weston, 1992, p. xi). Here is the argument reduced to its components:

- *Conclusion:* If we prescribe Ritalin for Willie, his academic performance will improve.
- *Premise:* Willie has an attention-deficit hyperactivity disorder.
- *Premise:* This disorder decreases academic performance.
- *Premise:* Ritalin reduces hyperactivity in school children.
- *Warrant:* (evidence regarding the truth of a premise) It is assumed that there is empirical evidence that children who take

Ritalin have better long-term academic performance than those who do not. Weber, et al., 1992, argue that there is counter-evidence regarding this claim.

If a claim is made and no reason, piece of evidence, or statement of support accompanies it, then there is no argument. Many editorials and letters to the editor have a point to make but no arguments: They give no reasons for the position taken. It is not a mistake to have strong views. The mistake is to have nothing else (Weston, 1992, p. xi). General rules for composing arguments include the following:

1. Distinguish between premises and conclusion
2. Present your ideas in a natural order
3. Start from reliable premises
4. Use definite, specific, concrete language
5. Avoid loaded language
6. Use consistent terms
7. Stick to one meaning for each term (Weston, 1992, p. v).

An argument may be unsound because there is something wrong with its logical structure, because it contains false premises, or because it is irrelevant to the claim or is circular. Anthony Weston suggests that basing conclusions on too little evidence (e.g., generalizing from incomplete information) and overlooking alternatives are perhaps the two greatest fallacies.

Guidelines for Evaluating Arguments*

A first step in evaluating arguments is to identify which of several statements in a piece of writing or discourse is the conclusion. The conclusion of an argument should be the statement or claim that has at least one other statement in support of it. In a long argument, there may be more than one conclusion. More than one argument may be presented. If so, treat each argument separately. Remember, opinions are not arguments.

There are four general criteria of a good argument: (1) the premises are *relevant* to the truth of the conclusion; (2) they are *acceptable;* (3) when viewed together the premises constitute *sufficient grounds* for the truth of the conclusion; and (4) the premises provide an *effective rebuttal* to all reasonable challenges to the argument. An argument that violates any one of these criteria is flawed.

1. *The Relevance Criterion.* The premises must be *relevant* to the conclusion. A premise is relevant if it makes a difference to the truth or falsity of the conclusion. A premise is irrelevant if its acceptance has no bearing on the truth or falsity of the conclusion. In most cases, the relevance of a premise is also determined by its relation to other premises. In some cases, additional premises may be needed to make the relevance of another premise apparent.

---

*This section is based on *Attacking Faulty Reasoning: A Practical Guide to Fallacy-Free Arguments* (pp. 12–16) by T. E. Damer, 1995, Belmont, CA: Wadsworth. Copyright 1995 by Wadsworth Publishing Co. Reprinted by permission.

2. *The Acceptability Criterion.* The premises must be acceptable. The term *acceptable* is preferable to the more traditional term *true*. Acceptability means that which a reasonable person *should* accept. A premise is *acceptable* if it reflects any of the following:

- A claim that is a matter of undisputed common knowledge
- A claim that is adequately defended in the same discussion or at least capable of being adequately defended on request or with further inquiry
- A conclusion of another good argument
- An uncontroverted eyewitness testimony
- An uncontroverted report from an expert in the field

A premise is *unacceptable* if it reflects any of the following:

- A claim that contradicts any of the following: the evidence, a well-established claim, a reliable source, or other premises in the same argument
- A questionable claim that is not adequately defended in the context of the discussion or in some other accessible source
- A claim that is self-contradictory, linguistically confusing, or otherwise unintelligible
- A claim that is no different from, or that is as questionable as, the conclusion that it is supposed to support
- A claim that is based on a usually unstated but highly questionable assumption or an unacceptable premise

The premises of an argument should be regarded as acceptable if each meets at least one of the conditions of acceptability and if none meet a condition of unacceptability.

3. *The Sufficient Grounds Criterion.* The premises of a good argument must provide *sufficient grounds* for the truth of its conclusion. If the premises are not sufficient in number, kind, and weight, they may not be strong enough to establish the conclusion, even though they may be both relevant and acceptable. Additional relevant and acceptable premises may be needed to make the case. This is perhaps the most difficult criterion to apply, because there are not clear guidelines to help us determine what constitutes sufficient grounds for the truth of a claim or the rightness of an action. Argumentative contexts differ and thus create different sufficiency demands. There are many ways that arguments may fail to satisfy the sufficiency criterion:

- A premise may be based on a small or unrepresentative sample. For example, a premise may rely on anecdotal data (e.g., the personal experience of the arguer or of a few people of his or her acquaintance).
- A premise might be based on a faulty causal analysis.
- Crucial evidence may be missing.

4. *The Rebuttal Criterion.* A good argument should provide an *effective rebuttal* to the strongest arguments against your

conclusion and the strongest arguments in support of alternative positions. A good argument, usually presented in relation to another side to the issue, must meet that other side head-on. Most people can devise what *appears* to be a good argument for whatever it is that they want to believe or want others to believe. There cannot be good arguments in support of both sides of opposing or contradictory positions, because at least half the arguments presented will not be able to satisfy the rebuttal criterion.

The ultimate key to distinguishing between a good and a mediocre argument is how well the rebuttal criterion has been met. Rebuttal is frequently neglected for several reasons. First, people may not discover any good answers to challenges to their position, so they just keep quiet about them. Second, they may not want to mention the contrary evidence for fear that their position will be weakened by bringing it to the attention of opponents.Finally, they may be so convinced by their own position that they don't believe that there is another side to the issue. Good arguers examine counterexamples as well as examples compatible with their claim. They look at all the evidence. As a critical thinker, you cannot discount information simply because it conflicts with your opinions.

INSTRUCTIONS

1. Review the guidelines for evaluating arguments.
2. Locate a brief argument. Make a copy of this so it is readily available.
3. Review the argument you will analyze.
4. Complete the Argument Analysis Form in Exhibit 19.1.
5. Exchange your argument analysis with another student.

FOLLOW-UP QUESTIONS

1. What was the most difficult part of completing your argument analysis?

   _____

   _____

   _____

   _____

   _____

2. Did you come up with effective rebuttals to your argument?

   _____

   _____

   _____

   _____

Exhibit 19.1   **ARGUMENT ANALYSIS FORM**

Your Name   Date

Course

Instructor's Name

Select a practice-related argument. We recommend a short one made up of just a few sentences. Longer statements become complex quickly. Attach a copy to this form.

1. State each element of the argument.
    Conclusion:

    _____

    _____

    Hint: It might be easiest to identify the conclusion first. Longer arguments often have more than one conclusion.

    Premise 1:

    _____

    _____

    Premise 2:

    _____

    _____

    Premise 3:

    _____

    _____

                                        (There may be more.)
    Warrants for each premise (if relevant):

    _____

    _____

    _____

2. Examine each premise, using the following criteria and write your answers below, including the reasons for them.

- Is it relevant? (Does it have a bearing on whether the conclusion is true?) If so, explain how.

_____

_____

_____

_____

- Is it acceptable? (Would a reasonable person accept it?)

_____

_____

_____

_____

- Does it provide sufficient grounds? If so, explain how.

_____

_____

_____

_____

- Can you provide an effective rebuttal to counterarguments? If yes, describe the strongest counterargument as well as your rebuttal.

_____

_____

_____

_____

_____

_____

_____

_____

_____

_____

_____

_____

Exercise 20
THINKING CRITICALLY ABOUT CASE RECORDS

PURPOSE

To increase your skills in preparing and critiquing case records.

BACKGROUND

Professional practice requires preparing and reviewing case records. Social workers spend considerable time recording. Recording should contribute to effective service. Records help to avoid mistakes based on faulty recollections and can be useful in planning service and reviewing progress. Reviews of case records reveal many deficiencies (Tallant, 1988), which include unnecessary repetition, missing data, and poor organization (see Exhibit 20.1). Case records are most likely to be useful if they have certain characteristics (e.g., clearly describe problems and related circumstances) (see Exhibit 20.2). Record-writing tips include the following:

- Be precise.
- Get rid of unnecessary words.
- Use active rather than passive verbs.
- Define terms clearly.
- Focus on main points.
- Identify conclusions and premises clearly.

Rules of thumb such as asking, "Is this material useful?" can help you to decide what to record. Well-designed forms will facilitate the recording and review of material.

INSTRUCTIONS

1. Select a detailed case study presented in the professional literature (or use a record given to you by your instructor). Rate it with the list of guidelines in Exhibit 20.2. (You could also note practitioner fallacies and their frequency, e.g., ad hominem argument, appeals to authority.)
2. Determine your overall score: _____
   (Scores range from 0 to 66.)
3. Be prepared to describe the rationale for your ratings.
4. Select an example of a service agreement and review this based on the list in Exhibit 20.3.

5. Determine an overall summary score: _____
   (Scores range from 0 to 15.)
6. Be prepared to describe the rationale for your rating.

FOLLOW-UP QUESTIONS

1. How does this exercise apply to written service agreements with clients?

_____

_____

_____

_____

_____

_____

_____

2. What problems are common in your agency's records?

_____

_____

_____

_____

_____

_____

_____

_____

Exhibit 20.1

Common Problems with Case Records

- Emphasizing assumed pathology of clients and significant others and overlooking client assets
- Vague descriptions of problems and related circumstances
- Incomplete assessment (e.g., environmental causes are overlooked)
- Missing demographic information (e.g., household members)
- Inclusion of irrelevant content
- Unsupported speculation
- Use of jargon, psychobabble (vague, ambiguous terms)
- Conclusions based on small, biased samples
- Descriptive terms used as explanations
- Vague description of assessment methods
- Vague description of intervention methods
- Vague description of goals and related objectives
- Missing information about recent service and progress

Exhibit 20.2   **GUIDELINES FOR REVIEWING CASE RECORDS**

Your Name _____   Date _____

Course _____

Instructor's Name _____

	NOT AT ALL	SOMEWHAT	MOSTLY	COMPLETELY
1. Demographic data are complete.	0	1	2	3
2. Presenting problems are clearly noted.	0	1	2	3
3. An overview of problems (desired outcomes) is included.	0	1	2	3
4. Presenting problems (desired outcomes) are clearly described.[a]	0	1	2	3
5. Circumstances related to behaviors of concern are clearly described.[b]	0	1	2	3
6. Baseline levels of problem-related behaviors are described.	0	1	2	3
7. Sources of assessment data are noted.	0	1	2	3
8. Self-report is complemented by observational data.	0	1	2	3
9. Relevant historical information is included.	0	1	2	3
10. Collected data are clearly summarized.	0	1	2	3
11. Relevant client assets are clearly described.	0	1	2	3
12. Environmental resources are clearly described.	0	1	2	3
13. Specific objectives related to each problem as well as intermediate steps are clearly described.[c]	0	1	2	3
14. Uninformative labels are avoided.	0	1	2	3
15. Inferences about causes of problems are well reasoned (logically and empirically).	0	1	2	3
16. There is little irrelevant material (content with no intervention guidelines).	0	1	2	3
17. Intervention methods are clearly described.	0	1	2	3
18. Degree of progress is clearly noted, based on ongoing monitoring of specific, relevant progress indicators.	0	1	2	3
19. A log of contacts is included.	0	1	2	3
20. Content is up-to-date.	0	1	2	3
21. Handwriting is easy to read.	0	1	2	3
22. Report is well organized.	0	1	2	3

[a]Clear description includes a description of the form of related behaviors, feelings, and thoughts as well as their duration, their frequency or rate (as relevant), and the situations in which they occur.
[b]Including relevant antecedents, consequences, and setting events.
[c]A clear description includes what is to be done and when, where, by whom, and how often.

Exhibit 20.3 **GUIDELINES FOR REVIEWING SERVICE AGREEMENTS**

Your Name   Date

Course

Instructor's Name

	NOT AT ALL	SOMEWHAT	MOSTLY	COMPLETELY
1. An overall service goal is noted (if relevant).	0	1	2	3
2. Objectives related to the goal are clearly described.	0	1	2	3
3. Participants are clearly noted.	0	1	2	3
4. The consequences of meeting (or not meeting) objectives are clearly described.	0	1	2	3
5. The form is signed by all participants.	0	1	2	3

Overall critique*

_____

_____

_____

_____

_____

_____

_____

_____

_____

_____

_____

*Attach a copy of service agreement (as relevant).

5 REVIEWING EDUCATIONAL AND PRACTICE ENVIRONMENTS

The two exercises included in Part 5 will help you to apply critical thinking to your work and educational environments. Exercise 21 contains a checklist you can use to explore the extent to which your work environment offers a culture of thoughtfulness. Exercise 22 provides a measure you can use to evaluate the extent to which instructors encourage critical thinking.

Formidable obstacles lie ahead for those who resolve to think critically in their practice. Our students, who confront these obstacles for the first time in their fieldwork and professional practice, often report a mixture of amazement, discomfort, aloneness, and feeling out of step as they try to exercise their critical thinking skills. To help you prepare for this experience, we have asked two of our recently graduated students to report on their initial experiences as a critical thinker in social-work practice.

Polly Doud, who graduated from the University of Wisconsin—Eau Claire in 1992, described events during a hospital case conference involving social workers, nurses, and a physician. She identified the problem as an "appeal to authority." In this instance, the nurses and social workers had carefully examined the evidence about a patient's care and had arrived at a consensus. The doctor entered the room and, after a superficial examination of the patient's situation, decided on a course of action. Polly said, "If the nurses and social workers, myself included, had spoken up about the things that we had brought up before the authority had walked in the room, I think that things would have been a lot different." Polly was concerned because accepting the doctor's conclusion, without counterargument, may have jeopardized patient care.

Sandra Willoughby, another University of Wisconsin—Eau Claire student who graduated in 1993, described events during an inservice training session for professional helpers that was conducted by a woman advocating "alternative therapies" including "feeling/touch" and "art therapy" as treatments for women in a refuge house for battered women. Sandra entered the conference room "really planning to go in and question her methods."

The presenter never referred to data regarding effectiveness, nor to studies evaluating it; she advocated for her treatment methods based on "her own personal experience with suffering and long depression and her own having lived through pain so that she can identify with clients, and therefore, help them."

Sandra felt uncomfortable asking for evidence about the method's effectiveness because "We had all gone around and introduced ourselves before the speaker began talking, and they were all therapists and professionals in the field, and I introduced myself as a 'student,' so I also felt, 'Who am I to say anything?'"

Sandra also felt uncomfortable asking about effectiveness because "I'm looking around the room at the other professionals and I'm noticing a lot of 'nodding' and nonverbals that say, 'Oh yeah, that's great and everything.'"

Sandra also "sensed from her [the presenter] a lot of vulnerability, and she even almost teared up a couple of times." When the presentation was over, Sandra's colleagues did not ask a single question about effectiveness, but asked only "supportive questions like, 'How do we refer clients to you?'" Sandra said,

> How can I ask the question that I want to ask but in a safe way? Feeling very uncomfortable, I did end up asking her. She talked [in response to Sandra's question about effectiveness] a lot about spiritual emergence as a phenomenon that people go through and how she helps them through this. . . . She kept using 'spiritual emergence' over and over again without defining it. . . . She just described why she does it [the treatment] as far as energy fields in the body.

Sandra concluded from the experience that "This is not typical among professionals [asking whether the method works and how this is known]. . . . It's not commonplace."

We think that Sandra's experience may be common in social work. She is the first of our students in over a decade who has attended a professional conference—often these conferences are attended by hundreds —or an inservice who has asked, "Is your method effective? How do you know?"

Here is the lesson from all this: Expect to be out of step. Expect to feel uncomfortable as a critical thinker. Expect to encounter the perception that you are somehow odd, insensitive, and cynical if you ask about a method's effectiveness, but take heart from knowing that if you truly want to help clients, you will ask for evidence that can point the way toward helping, not hurting or accomplishing nothing. The difference between students like Polly and Sandra, compared with other social work students who are not trained in critical thinking, lies in their commitment to critical discussion that will better serve clients.

Exercise 21
ENCOURAGING A CULTURE OF THOUGHTFULNESS

PURPOSE

This exercise provides an opportunity to review the quality of your work environment as a first step toward identifying constructive changes that you and your colleagues could pursue.

BACKGROUND

The environments in which we work influence our decisions. These environments may encourage or discourage critical thinking which, in turn, will influence the quality of practice decisions.

INSTRUCTIONS

1. Complete the Culture of Thoughtfulness Scale in Exhibit 21.1.
2. Give your total score. The range of scores is 24 to 120.

Score = _____

3. If your score falls below 100, select two characteristics you want to improve and write their numbers here:

_____ and _____

For each, describe exactly how such improvement could enhance the quality of thoughtfulness in your work environment as well as how you could seek this change.

Plan for Number _____ :

_____

_____

_____

Why would this change be beneficial?

_____

_____

Plan for Number _____ :

_____

_____

_____

_____

_____

Why would this change be beneficial?

_____

_____

_____

_____

_____

_____

_____

_____

_____

4. If your score was 100 or above, describe two ways you could maintain the culture of thoughtfulness.

_____

_____

_____

_____

_____

_____

_____

_____

_____

_____

_____

_____

_____

Exhibit 21.1   **CULTURE OF THOUGHTFULNESS SCALE**

Your Name _____   Date _____

Course _____

Instructor's Name _____

Please circle the numbers in the columns that best describe your responses.

SD = Strongly Disagree   **D** = Disagree   **N** = Neither   **A** = Agree   **SA** = Strongly Agree

No.	Statements Describing Actions in Your Work Environment	SD	D	N	A	SA
1.	The purposes of discussions are clearly described.	1	2	3	4	5
2.	Alternative views on issues are sought.	1	2	3	4	5
3.	Alternative views are considered carefully.	1	2	3	4	5
4.	Evidence against as well as for favored views is sought.	1	2	3	4	5
5.	Key terms are clearly defined.	1	2	3	4	5
6.	Behaviors of interest are clearly described, with specific examples given.	1	2	3	4	5
7.	Questions are clearly stated.	1	2	3	4	5
8.	People identify assumptions underlying their beliefs.	1	2	3	4	5
9.	Implications of proposed options are clearly described.	1	2	3	4	5
10.	Getting at the "truth" is valued over "winning" an argument.	1	2	3	4	5
11.	People are never punished for introducing ideas that differ from those favored by a group.	1	2	3	4	5
12.	Criticisms of an argument focus on important points and are made without sarcasm or put-downs.	1	2	3	4	5
13.	When available and relevant, research data are cited in support of statements and related sources are noted; appropriate documentation is provided.	1	2	3	4	5
14.	Inferences made are compatible with what is known about behavior.	1	2	3	4	5
15.	Group leaders/administrators do not rely on unsupported pronouncements about what is best.	1	2	3	4	5
16.	Beliefs and actions are well reasoned (based on acceptable, relevant, and sufficient evidence).	1	2	3	4	5
17.	The buddy-buddy system (agreement based on friendship rather than the cogency of a view) is discouraged.	1	2	3	4	5

(continued)

Exhibit 21.1
(continued)

No.	Statements Describing Actions in Your Work Environment	SD	D	N	A	SA
18.	Participants do not interrupt each other.	1	2	3	4	5
19.	People take responsibility for describing the reasons for their beliefs/actions.	1	2	3	4	5
20.	People change their mind when there is good reason to do so.	1	2	3	4	5
21.	Participants thank others who point out errors in their thinking.	1	2	3	4	5
22.	Reliance on questionable criteria is avoided (e.g., unfounded authority, tradition, anecdotal experience).*	1	2	3	4	5
23.	Diversionary tactics are avoided (e.g., red herring, angering an opponent).*	1	2	3	4	5
24.	Evasive tactics are avoided (e.g., changing the topic).*	1	2	3	4	5

SD = Strongly Disagree   **D** = Disagree   **N** = Neither   **A** = Agree   **SA** = Strongly Agree

*You could use Cells 22–24 to determine the rate per minute of informal fallacies during a discussion.

FOLLOW-UP QUESTIONS

1. Which three items (highest scores) are your workplace's greatest strengths?

   a. _____

   _____

   b. _____

   _____

   c. _____

   _____

2. Which three items (lowest scores) are your workplace's greatest weaknesses?

   a. _____

   _____

   b. _____

   _____

   c. _____

   _____

3. What is the usual fallacy rate in case conferences? Identify key fallacies of interest, drawing on fallacies described in Part 3. Keep track of how often each occurs during case conferences. To determine the rate, divide each by the number of minutes observed to determine the rate per minute.

Fallacies selected   *Rate*

1. _____   _____

2. _____   _____

3. _____   _____

4. You could also select items from Exhibit 21.1 and keep track of their rate during staff meetings or case conferences.

Indicators selected   *Rate*

1. _____   _____

2. _____   _____

3. _____   _____

4. _____   _____

Exercise 22
EVALUATING THE TEACHING OF CRITICAL-THINKING SKILLS

PURPOSE

This exercise provides an opportunity to assess the extent to which an instructor teaches critical-thinking skills.

BACKGROUND

Classrooms vary widely in the extent to which critical-thinking skills are taught. The Teaching Evaluation Form (Exhibit 22.1) included in this exercise consists of thirty-five statements about your instructor's teaching style related to critical thinking. The statements were developed in collaboration with Professor-Emeritus Michael Hakeem of the University of Wisconsin—Madison. The statements have not been subjected to any item analysis, nor have reliability or validity checks been done, so we know little of the instrument's measurement properties. For example, a question to be pursued is, Do students who rate their instructors high on teaching critical thinking learn more related skills compared with students who rate their instructors low?

INSTRUCTIONS

1. Do not put your name on the form (Exhibit 22.1).
2. Please circle each answer that most accurately describes the extent to which you agree or disagree with the statement. Leave none blank.
3. When you are finished, score your answers based on the instructions given on p. 228 and record the score at the bottom of the form.

Exhibit 22.1   **TEACHING EVALUATION FORM**

Course _____   Date _____

Instructor's Name _____

Please circle the numbers in the columns that best describe your responses.

	SD = Strongly Disagree **D** = Disagree **N** = Neutral **A** = Agree **SA** = Strongly Agree					
No.	Statements Describing Instructor's Critical-Thinking Teaching Style	SD	D	N	A	SA
1.	The instructor regularly presents arguments for and against controversial issues presented in class.	1	2	3	4	5
2.	The instructor usually does not define major terms used in the class.	1	2	3	4	5
3.	The instructor regularly refers to documentation (e.g., cites studies to support conclusions.	1	2	3	4	5
4.	The instructor usually does not determine where students stand on a particular issue before presenting arguments and counterarguments regarding that issue.	1	2	3	4	5
5.	The instructor teaches students how to pose clear questions for themselves.	1	2	3	4	5
6.	The instructor *does not* teach students how to find evidence for themselves about the topic under discussion.	1	2	3	4	5
7.	The instructor *does not* teach students procedures for answering their own questions.	1	2	3	4	5
8.	The instructor rewards students for coming to their own well-reasoned conclusions, rather than simply rewarding them for agreeing.	1	2	3	4	5
9.	The instructor's way of teaching leads students to understand principles that are generally applicable to other situations.	1	2	3	4	5
10.	The instructor "sells" a particular point of view.	1	2	3	4	5
11.	The instructor's examinations require memorizing key points.	1	2	3	4	5
12.	The instructor *does not* let you know how his or her conclusions were reached.	1	2	3	4	5
13.	The instructor's assignments emphasize how to think through things for yourself rather than memorization.	1	2	3	4	5
14.	The instructor teaches skills and techniques that will be useful for solving problems in practice.	1	2	3	4	5
15.	The instructor gives specific examples to illustrate and explain content in the course.	1	2	3	4	5

(continued)

Exhibit 22.1
(continued)

		SD = Strongly Disagree	D = Disagree	N = Neutral	A = Agree		SA = Strongly Agree		
No.	Statements Describing Instructor's Critical-Thinking Teaching Style				SD	D	N	A	SA
16.	Generally, no matter what evidence you could present to the instructor, the instructor's conclusions would be unchanged.				1	2	3	4	5
17.	The instructor encourages students to be skeptical about conclusions.				1	2	3	4	5
18.	If the instructor had drawn a conclusion about a particular topic, and a student presented documentation to the contrary, the instructor would thank the student.				1	2	3	4	5
19.	The instructor rewards students for learning how to think for themselves.				1	2	3	4	5
20.	The instructor teaches that all conclusions are equally valid.				1	2	3	4	5
21.	The instructor shows students the specific steps that were followed to draw important conclusions in the course.				1	2	3	4	5
22.	The instructor never mentions that current views taught in the course may be found to be false.				1	2	3	4	5
23.	Where appropriate, the instructor gives students measures to define key concepts.				1	2	3	4	5
24.	The instructor identifies underlying assumptions related to conclusions.				1	2	3	4	5
25.	The instructor relies on case examples rather than data to provide evidence for claims and arguments.				1	2	3	4	5
26.	The instructor relies on his or her personal experience to support claims and conclusions.				1	2	3	4	5
27.	The instructor encourages students to base their conclusions on sound documentation (studies, original observations, data).				1	2	3	4	5
28.	The instructor makes fun of those who disagree with his or her position.				1	2	3	4	5
29.	The instructor assigns readings that argue for and against important points in the course.				1	2	3	4	5
30.	The instructor assigns readings that generally support one particular point of view.				1	2	3	4	5
31.	The instructor thinks that data are all right as long as they support a particular conclusion.				1	2	3	4	5
32.	The instructor emphasizes the value of finding out what is true rather than how to "win" an argument.				1	2	3	4	5
33.	The instructor teaches how to find truth for yourself.				1	2	3	4	5
34.	The instructor tells you what the truth is and expects you to agree.				1	2	3	4	5
35.	The instructor would smile in satisfaction if a student cited a study that disagrees with a claim that the instructor presented.				1	2	3	4	5

Scoring: Add the weights for items 1, 3, 5, 8, 9, 13, 14, 15, 17, 18, 19, 21, 23, 24, 27, 29, 32, 33, and 35.

SCORE *(Range: 35–175)*

Subtotal = _____

Reverse the weights for the following items and add them: 2, 4, 6, 7, 10, 11, 12, 16, 20, 22, 25, 26, 28, 30, 31, 34.

Subtotal = _____

Total = _____

1. Which item seems most important as a characteristic for an instructor who teaches critical thinking?

_____

_____

_____

_____

_____

_____

_____

2. Which item seems least important as a characteristic for an instructor who teaches critical thinking?

_____

_____

_____

_____

_____

_____

REFERENCES

ABRAHAM, I. L., & SCHULTZ, S. (1984). The "law of small numbers": An unexpected and incidental replication. *The Journal of Psychology, 117,* 183–188.

ALLEN, R. W., & GREENE, L. (1975). *Propaganda game.* New Haven, CT: Autotelic Instructional Materials.

AMERICAN PSYCHIATRIC ASSOCIATION (1994). *Diagnostic and statistical manual of mental disorders* (4th ed.). American Psychiatric Association: Washington, DC.

ANASTASI, A. (1989). *Psychological testing* (6th ed.). New York: Macmillan.

APFEL, R. J., & FISHER, S. M. (1984). *Do no harm: DES and the dilemmas of modern medicine.* New Haven, CT: Yale University Press.

ARKAVA, M. I., & LANE, T. A. (1983). *Beginning social work research.* Newton, MA: Allyn and Bacon.

ARKES, H. R. (1981). Impediments to accurate clinical judgment and possible way to minimize their impact. *Journal of Consulting and Clinical Psychology, 49*(3), 323–330.

ASIMOV, I. (1989). The relativity of wrong. *Skeptical Inquirer, 14,* 35–44.

ATHERTON, C. R., & KLEMMACK, D. L. (1982). *Research methods in social work.* Lexington, MA: D. C. Heath.

BADGER, D. (1985). Learning for transfer: A further contribution. *Issues in Social Work Education. 5*(1), 63–66.

BARNETT, E. (1986). *Staff patterns in mental health agencies and organizations.* Alexandria, VA: American Association for Counseling and Development, American Counseling Association.

BARON, J. (1985). *Rationality and intelligence.* New York: Cambridge University Press.

BARON, J. (1994). *Thinking and deciding* (2nd ed.). Cambridge, England: Cambridge University Press.

BELSON, W. A. (1981). *The design and understanding of survey questions.* Aldershot, Hants, England: Gower.

BERENDES, H. W., & LEE, Y. H. (1993). The 1953 clinical trial of diethylstilbestrol during pregnancy: Could it have stopped DES use? *Controlled Clinical Trials, 14,* 179–182.

BERGER, R. & PILIAVIN, I. (1976). The effect of casework: A research note. *Social Work, 21,* 205–208.

BERKOW, R., & FLETCHER, A. J. (Eds.). (1987). *The Merck manual.* Rahway, NJ: Merck & Co.

BIRD, F., DORES, P. A., MONIZ, D., & ROBINSON, J. (1989). Reducing severe aggressive and self-injurious behaviors with functional communication training. *American Journal of Mental Retardation, 94*(1), 37–48.

BISHOP, J. M. (1984). Infuriating tensions: Science and the medical student. *Journal of Medical Education, 59,* 91–102.

BLENKNER, M., BLOOM, M., & NIELSEN, M. (1971). A research and demonstration project of protective services. *Social Casework, 52*(8), 483–499.

BLENNER, J. L. (1991). Researcher for a day: A simulation game. *Nurse Educator, 16*(2), 32–35.

BOSK, C. L. (1979). *Forgive and remember: Managing medical failure.* Chicago: University of Chicago Press.

BREGGIN, P. R. (1991). *Toxic psychiatry.* New York: St. Martin's Press.

BROOKFIELD, S. D. (1987). *Developing critical thinkers.* San Francisco: Jossey-Bass.

BROWNE, M. N., & KEELEY, S. M. (1994). *Asking the right questions: A guide to critical thinking* (4th ed.). Englewood Cliffs, NJ: Prentice-Hall.

BUNGE, M. (1984). What is pseudoscience? *The Skeptical Inquirer, 9*(1), 36–47.

BURNHAM, J. (1987). *Why superstition won and science lost.* New Brunswick, NJ: Rutgers University Press.

CANNELL, C. F., LAWSON, S. A., & HAUSSER, D. L. (1975). *A technique for evaluating interviewer performance.* Ann Arbor, MI: University of Michigan, Survey Research Center of the Institute for Social Research.

CAPALDI, N. (1979). *The art of deception* (2nd ed.).Buffalo, NY: Prometheus Press.

CECI, S. J., & BRUCK, M. (1993). Suggestibility of the child witness: A historical review and synthesis. *Psychological Bulletin, 113*(3), 403–439.

CHAFFEE, J. (1988). *Thinking critically.* Boston: Houghton Mifflin.

CHASE, S. (1956). *Guides to straight thinking.* New York: Harper & Row.

CIALDINI, R. B. (1984). *Influence: The new psychology of modern persuasion.* New York: Quill.

CLANCY, C. M., CEBUL, R. D., & WILLIAMS, S. V. (1988). Guiding individual decisions: A randomized, controlled trial of decision analysis. *American Journal of Medicine, 84,* 238–288.

COHEN, J. (1977). *Statistical power analysis for the behavioral sciences* (Rev. ed.). New York: Academic Press.

CONROY, D. L. (1991). *Out of the nightmare: Recovery from depression and suicidal pain.* New York: New Liberty.

COOK, T. D., & CAMPBELL, D. T. (1979). *Quasi-experimentation: Design and analysis issues for field settings.* Boston: Houghton Mifflin.

CORCORAN, S. A., & TANNER, C. (1988). Implications of clinical judgment research for teaching. In National League for Nursing, *Curriculum resolution: Mandate for change* (pp. 159–176). New York: National League for Nursing.

CORMIER, S. M., & HAGMAN, J. D. (1987). *Transfer of learning: Contemporary research and applications.* San Diego, CA: Academic Press.

COUNCIL ON SOCIAL WORK EDUCATION. (1992). *Curriculum policy statement for baccalaureate degree programs in social work education.* Alexandria, VA.

COUSINS, P. S., FISCHER, J. GLISSON, C., & KAMEOKA, V. (1986). The effects of physical attractiveness and verbal expressiveness on clinical judgments. *Journal of Social Service Research, 8*(4), 59–74.

CRAMP, A. J., & SIMMONS, G. H. (1936). *Nostrums and quackery and pseudo-medicine* (Vol. 3). Chicago: American Medical Association.

CRUMB, F. W. (1973). Boos and bouquets for Fischer [letter to the editor]. *Social Work, 18*(2), 124, 126.

DAMER, T. E. (1995). *Attacking faulty reasoning: A practical guide to fallacy-free argument* (3rd ed.). Belmont, CA: Wadsworth.

DAWES, R. M. (1988). *Rational choice in an uncertain world.* San Diego, CA: Harcourt Brace Jovanovich.

DAWES, R. M. (1994a). *House of cards: Psychology and psychotherapy built on myth.* New York: Free Press.

DAWES, R. M. (1994b). On the necessity of examining all four cells in a 2 × 2 table. *Making Better Decisions, 1*(2), 2–4. Pacific Grove, CA: Brooks/Cole.

DAWES, R. M., FAUST, D., & MEEHL, P. E. (1989). Clinical versus actuarial judgment. *Science, 243,* 1668–1673.

DEAN, G. (1986–1987). Does astrology need to be true? Part 1: A look at the real thing. *The Skeptical Inquirer, 11*(2), 166–185.

DEAN, G. (1987). Does astrology need to be true? Part 2: The answer is no. *The Skeptical Inquirer, 11*(3), 257–273.

DEWEY, J. (1933). *How we think: A restatement of the relation of reflective thinking to the educative process.* Boston: Heath.

DINGWALL, R., EEKELAR, J., & MURPHY, T. (1983). *The protection of children.* Oxford, England: Basil Blackwell.

DOWDEN, B. H. (1993). *Logical reasoning.* Belmont, CA: Wadsworth.

DRUCKMAN, D., & BJORK, R. A. (Eds.). (1991). *In the mind's eye: Enhancing human performance.* Washington, DC: National Academy Press.

DUTTON, D. B. (1988). *Worse than the disease: Pitfalls of medical progress.* New York: Cambridge University Press.

EDDY, D. M. (1982). Probabalistic reasoning in clinical medicine: Problems and opportunities. D. Kahneman, P. Slovic, & A. Tversky (Eds.), *Judgment under uncertainty: Heuristics and biases* (pp. 249–267). Cambridge, England: Cambridge University Press.

EINHORN, H. J., & HOGARTH, R. M. (1986). Judging probable cause. *Psychological Bulletin, 99*(1), 3–19.

ELLUL, J. (1965). *Propaganda: The formation of men's attitudes.* New York: Vintage.

ELSTEIN, A. S. (1989). Decision analysis in surgical education. *World Journal of Surgery, 1*(3), 287–291.

ELSTEIN, A. S., DAWSON-SAUNDERS, B., & BELZER, L. J. (1985). Instruction in medical decision making: A report of two surveys. *Medical Decision Making, 5*(2), 229–233.

ELSTEIN, A. S., SCHULMAN, L. W., SPRAFKA, S. A., ALLAL, L., GORDON, M., JASON, H., KAGAN, N., LOUPE, M., & JORDAN, R. (1978). *Medical problem solving: An analysis of clinical reasoning.* Cambridge, MA: Harvard University Press.

ENGEL, S. M. (1994). *With good reason: An introduction to informal fallacies* (5th ed.). New York: St. Martin's Press.

ENNIS, R. H. (1987). A taxonomy of critical thinking dispositions and abilities. In J. B. Baron & R. J. Sternberg (Eds.), *Teaching thinking skills: theory and practice* (pp. 9–26). New York: W. H. Freeman.

EVANS, B. (1958). *The natural history of nonsense.* New York: Vintage.

FEARNSIDE, W. W., & HOLTHER, W. B. (1959). *Fallacy: The counterfeit of argument.* Englewood Cliffs, NJ: Prentice-Hall.

FINCKENAUER, J. O. (1982). *Scared Straight! and the panacea phenomenon.* Englewood Cliffs, NJ: Rutgers University Press.

FINNEY, J. W., & MOOS, R. H. (1986). Matching patients with treatments: Conceptual and methodological issues. *Journal of Studies on Alcohol, 47*(2), 122–134.

FISCHER, J. (1973). Is casework effective?: A review. *Social Work. 18*(1), 5–20.

FISCHER, J. (1978). *Effective casework practice: An eclectic approach.* New York: McGraw-Hill.

FISCHER, J., & HUDSON, W. W. (1976). An effect of casework? Back to the drawing board. *Social Work, 21,* 347–349.

FISCHHOFF, B. (1975). Hindsight does not equal foresight: The effect of outcome knowledge on judgment under uncertainty. *Journal of Experimental Psychology, 1*(3), 288–299.

FISCHHOFF, B. (1977). Perceived informativeness of facts. *Journal of Experimental Psychology, Human Perception and Performance, 3,* 349–358.

FISCHHOFF, B., & BEYTH, R. (1975). "I knew it would happen." Remembered probabilities of once-future things. *Organizational Behavior and Human Performance, 13,* 1–16.

FONTEYN, M. E. (1991). Implications of clinical reasoning studies for critical care nursing. *Focus on Critical Care, 18*(4), 322–327.

FRANKLIN, D. L. (1986). Does client social class affect clinical judgement? *Social Casework, 67,* 424–432.

FREEDMAN, A. M., KAPLAN, H. I., & SADOCK, B. J. (1976). *Modern synopsis of psychiatry* (2nd ed.). Baltimore: Williams & Wilkins.

FREEMAN, J. B. (1993). *Thinking logically* (2nd ed.). Englewood Cliffs, NJ: Prentice-Hall.

GAMBRILL, E. (1990). *Critical thinking in clinical practice: Improving the accuracy of judgments and decisions about clients.* San Francisco: Jossey-Bass.

GAMBRILL, E. (1994). What critical thinking offers to clinicians. *The Behavior Therapist, 16*(6), 141–147.

GAMBRILL, E. (in press). *Social work practice: A critical thinker's guide.* White Plains, NY: Longman.

GARBARINO, J. (1992). *Children and families in the social environment* (2nd ed.). New York: Aldine de Gruyter.

GIBBS, L. E. (1983). Evaluation research: Scientist or advocate. *Journal of Social Service Research, 7*(1), 81–92.

GIBBS, L. E. (1989). The Quality of Study Rating Form: An instrument for synthesizing evaluation studies. *Journal of Social Work Education, 25*(1), 55–67.

GIBBS, L. E., (1991). *Scientific reasoning for social workers: Bridging the gap between research and practice.* New York: Macmillan.

GIBBS, L. E. (1994). Teaching clinical reasoning. *The Behavior Therapist, 17*(1), 1–6.

GIBBS, L. E., & JOHNSON, D. J. (1983). Computer assisted clinical decision making. *Journal of Social Service Research, 6*(3/4), 119–132.

GIBBS, L., GAMBRILL, E., BLAKEMORE, J., BEGUN, A., KENISTON, A., PEDEN, B., & LEFCOWITZ, M. (1995). A measure of critical thinking for practice. *Research on Social Work Practice, 5,* 193–204.

GIBELMAN, M., & SCHERVISH, P. H. (1993). *Who we are.* Washington, DC: National Association of Social Workers.

GLASS, G. V., & KLIEGEL, R. M. (1983). An apology for research integration in the study of psychotherapy. *Journal of Consulting and Clinical Psychology, 51*(1), 28–41.

GOVIER, T. (1985). *A practical study of argument.* Belmont, CA: Wadsworth.

GRAY, W. D. (1991). *Thinking critically about New Age ideas.* Belmont, CA: Wadsworth.

GREENO, J. G. (1989). A perspective on thinking. *American Psychologist, 2,* 131–141.

GRINNELL, R. M. (1985). *Social work research and evaluation* (2nd ed.). Itasca, IL: F. E. Peacock.

GRUENEICH, R. (1992). The borderline personality disorder diagnosis: Reliability, diagnostic efficiency, and covariation with other personality disorder diagnoses. *Journal of Personality Disorders, 8*(3), 197–212.

GUBERMAN, S. R., & GREENFIELD, P. M. (1991). Learning and transfer in everyday cognition. *Cognitive Development, 6,* 233–260.

GULA, R. J. (1979). *Nonsense: How to overcome it.* New York: Stein and Day.

HALEY, J. (1980). *Leaving home.* New York: McGraw-Hill.

HALLER, J. S. (1981). *American medicine in transition 1840–1910.* Urbana, IL: University of Illinois Press.

HALLINGER, P., & GREENBLATT, R. (1990). Designing professional development for transfer learning. *Planning and Changing, 21*(4), 195–206.

HAMILL, R., WILSON, T. D., & NISBETT, R. E. (1980). Insensitivity to sample bias: Generalizing from atypical cases. *Journal of Personality and Social Psychology, 39*(4), 578–589.

HANKS, H., HOBBS, C., & WYNNE, J. (1988). Early signs and recognition of sexual abuse in the pre-school child. In K. Browne, C. Davies, and P. Stratton (Eds.), *Early prediction and prevention of child abuse.* Chichester, England: John Wiley.

HARRIS, R. J. (1985). The transfer of learning in social work education. In R. J. Harris (Ed.), *Educating social workers* (pp. 80–91). Leicester, England: Association of Teachers in Social Work Education.

HAYS, W. L. (1981). *Statistics* (3rd ed.). New York: Holt, Rinehart & Winston.

HEALTH LETTER (1992). Only 750 restrictions on doctors' hospital privileges reported in the first year of data bank operation. *Health Letter, 8*(3), Published by Public Citizen Research Group, Washington, DC.

HERBERT, V. (1983). Special report on quackery: Nine ways to spot a quack! *Health, 15*(10), 39–41.

HOBBS, C. J., & WYNNE, J. M. (1986, October 4). Buggery in childhood: A common syndrome of child abuse. *The Lancet,* 792–796.

HOCH, L. (1971). Attitude change as a result of sex education. *Journal of Research in Science Teaching, 8,* 363–367.

HOFFMAN, P. (1986). *Predicting criminality* (Crime File Study Guide No. NCJ 97228). Rockville, MD: National Institute of Justice.

HOGARTH, R. M. (1987). *Judgment and choice* (2nd ed.). New York: Wiley.

HOLDEN, G., SPEEDLING, E., & ROSENBERG, G. (1992). Evaluation of an intervention designed to improve patients' hospital experience. *Psychological Reports, 71,* 547–550.

HOLLON, S. D., & KENDALL, P. C. (1980). Cognitive self-statements in depression: Development of an automatic thoughts questionnaire. *Cognitive Research and Therapy, 4,* 382–395.

HOWITT, D. (1992). *Child abuse errors: When good intentions go wrong.* New York: Harvester/Wheatsheaf.

HUCK, S. W., & SANDLER, H. M. (1979). *Rival hypotheses: Alternative interpretations of data based conclusions.* New York: Harper & Row.

ISEN, A. M. (1987). Positive affect, cognitive processes and social behavior. In L. Berkowitz (Ed.), *Advances in experimental social psychology* (Vol. 20). Orlando, FL: Academic Press.

JANIS, I. L. (1971, November). Groupthink. *Psychology Today, 5,* 43–46, 74–76.

JANIS, I. L. (1982). *Groupthink: Psychological studies of policy decisions and fiascoes* (2nd ed.). Boston: Houghton Mifflin.

JARVIS, W. (1987). Chiropractic: A skeptical view. *The Skeptical Inquirer, 12*(1), 47–55.

JARVIS, W. T. (1990). *Dubious dentistry.* Loma Linda, CA: Loma Linda University School of Medicine, Department of Public Health and Preventive Medicine.

JOHNSON, R. H., & BLAIR, J. A. (1983). *Logical self defense* (2nd ed.). Toronto: McGraw-Hill.

JOHNSON, S. M., KURTZ, M. E., TOMLINSON, T., & HOWE, K. R. (1986). Students' stereotypes of patients as barriers to clinical decision-making. *Journal of Medical Education, 61*(9), 727–735.

JOWETT, G. S., & O'DONNELL, V. (1992). *Propaganda and persuasion* (2nd ed.). Newbury Park, CA: Sage.

KADUSHIN, A. (1963). Diagnosis and evaluation for (almost) all occasions. *Social Work, 8*(1), 12–19.

KAGAN, R. M., REID, W. J., ROBERTS, S. E., & SILVERMAN-POLLOW, J. (1987). Engaging families of court-mandated youths in an alternative to institutional placement. *Child Welfare, 66*(4), 365–376.

KAHANE, H. (1992). *Logic and contemporary rhetoric: The use of reason in everyday life* (6th ed.). Belmont, CA: Wadsworth.

KAHNEMAN, D., SLOVIC, P., & TVERSKY, A. (1982). Judgment under uncertainty: Heuristics and biases. Cambridge, England: Cambridge University Press.

KASSIRER, J. P., & KOPELMAN, R. I. (1991). *Learning clinical reasoning.* Baltimore: Williams & Wilkins.

KERLINGER, F. N. (1986). *Foundations of behavioral research* (3rd ed.). New York: Holt, Rinehart & Winston.

KIRK, S. & KUTCHINS, H. (1992). *The selling of DSM: The rhetoric of science in psychiatry.* New York: Aldine de Gruyter.

KURTZ, M. E., JOHNSON, S. M., & RICE, S. (1989). Students' clinical assessments: Are they affected by stereotyping? *Journal of Social Work Education, 25*(1), 3–12.

KURTZ, R. M., & GARFIELD, S. L. (1978). Illusory correlation: A further exploration of Chapman's paradigm. *Journal of Consulting and Clinical Psychology, 46,* 1009–1015.

LANE, H. (1991). *The mask of benevolence: Disabling the deaf community.* New York: Random House.

LAZAR, A. (1991). Faculty, practitioner, and student attitudes toward research. *Journal of Social Work Education, 27*(1), 34–41.

LEAHEY, T. H., & LEAHEY, G. E. (1983). *Psychology's occult doubles: Psychology and the problem of pseudoscience.* Chicago: Nelson Hall.

LEE, A. M., & LEE, E. B. (1939). *The fine art of propaganda.* New York: Harcourt, Brace & Co.

LIPMAN, M. (1991). *Thinking in education.* Cambridge, England: Cambridge University Press.

Local lady took Natex year ago—had good health ever since. (1935, May 27). *Morning Call.* Allentown, PA, p. 7.

MALIVER, B. L. (1973). *The encounter game.* New York: Stein & Day.

MARSELLA, A. J. (1994). Depression. In R. J. Corsini (Ed.), *Encyclopedia of psychology* (pp. 399–402). New York: Wiley.

MARSH, H. W. (1987). Dr. Fox studies. *International Journal of Educational Research, 11,* 331–336.

MAYFIELD, M. (1991). *Thinking for yourself: Developing critical thinking skills through writing* (2nd ed.). Belmont, CA: Wadsworth.

MAYS, D. T., & FRANKS, C. M. (Eds.). (1985). *Negative outcome in psychotherapy and what to do about it.* New York: Springer.

MCCAIN, G., & SEGAL, E. M. (1988). *The game of science.* Pacific Grove, CA: Brooks/Cole.

MEDAWAR, P. B. (1967). *The art of the soluble.* London: Methuen.

MEEHL, P. E. (1973). Why I do not attend case conferences. In P. E. Meehl (Ed.), *Psychodiagnosis: Selected papers* (pp. 225–323), Minneapolis, MN: University of Minnesota Press.

MEIER, R. S., & FELDHUSEN, J. F. (1979). Another look at Dr. Fox: Effect of stated purpose for evaluation, lecturer expressiveness, and density of lecture content on student ratings. *Journal of Educational Psychology, 71,* 339–345.

MICHAEL, M., BOYCE, W. T., & WILCOX, A. J. (1984). *Biomedical bestiary: An epidemiologic guide to flaws and fallacies in the medical literature.* Boston: Little, Brown.

MILLER, A., ROBSON, D., & BUSHELL, R. (1986). Parental participation in paired reading: A controlled study. *Educational Psychology, 6*(3), 277–284.

MILLER, D. (1994). *Critical rationalism: A restatement and defense.* Chicago: Open Court.

MILLER, D. J., & HERSEN, M. (Eds.) (1992). *Research fraud in the behavioral and biomedical sciences.* New York: Wiley.

MILLER, S. I., & BOGAL, R. B. (1977). Logic as a tool for clinical training in social work. *Psychiatric Quarterly, 49*(1), 18–28.

MIROWSKY, J., & ROSS, C. E. (1989). *Social causes of psychological distress.* New York: Aldine de Gruyter.

MONTE, C. F. (1975). *Psychology's scientific endeavor.* New York: Praeger.

MOORE, B. N., & PARKER, R. (1986). *Critical thinking: Evaluating claims and arguments in everyday life.* Palo Alto, CA: Mayfield.

MORGAN, R. F. (1983). *The iatrogenics handbook: A critical look at research and practice in the helping professions.* Toronto, Canada: IPI Publishing Limited.

MOTTO, A. J., HEILBRON, D. C., & JUSTER, R. P. (1985). Development of a clinical instrument to estimate suicide risk. *American Journal of Psychiatry, 142*(6), 680–686.

NAFTULIN, D. H., WARE, J. E., & DONNELLY, F. A. (1973). The Doctor Fox lecture: A paradigm of educational seduction. *Journal of Medical Education, 48,* 630–635.

NATALE, J. A. (1988). Are you open to suggestion? *Psychology Today, 22,* 28–30.

NATIONAL ASSOCIATION OF SOCIAL WORKERS. (1987). *NASW standard for social work in health care settings.* Washington, DC: National Association of Social Workers.

NATIONAL ASSOCIATION OF SOCIAL WORKERS. (1990). *NASW clinical indicators for social work and psychosocial services in the acute psychiatric hospital.* Washington, DC: National Association of Social Workers.

NATIONAL ASSOCIATION OF SOCIAL WORKERS. (1991). *Standards of practice for social work mediators.* Washington, DC: National Association of Social Workers.

NICKERSON, R. S. (1986). *Reflections on reasoning.* Hillsdale, NJ: Erlbaum.

NICKERSON, R. S. (1988). On improving thinking through instruction. In E. Z. Rothkopf (Ed.), *Review of research in education, 15,* 3–57. Washington, DC: American Educational Research Association.

NICKERSON, R. S., PERKINS, D. N., & SMITH, E. E. (1985). *The teaching of thinking.* Hillsdale, NJ: Erlbaum.

NICOL, A. R., SMITH, J., KAY, B., HALL, D., BARLOW, J., & WILLIAMS, B. (1988). A focused casework approach to the treatment of child abuse: A controlled comparison. *Journal of Child Psychology and Psychiatry, 29*(5), 703–711.

NISBETT, R., & ROSS, L. (1980). *Human inference: Strategies and shortcomings in social judgment.* Englewood Cliffs, NJ: Prentice-Hall.

NISBETT, R. E., BORGIDA, E., CRANDALL, R., REED, H. (1982). In D. Kahneman, P. Slovic, & A. Tversky (Eds.), *Judgment under uncertainty: Heuristics and biases* (pp. 101–116). Cambridge, England: Cambridge University Press.

NORDHOLM, D. L. A. (1980). Beautiful patients are good patients: Evidence for the physical attractiveness stereotype in first impressions of patients. *Social Science and Medicine, 14A,* 81–83.

NORRIS, S. P. (1992). *The generalizability of critical thinking.* New York: Teachers College Press, Columbia University.

NURIUS, P. S. (1984). Utility of data synthesis for social work. *Social Work Research and Abstracts, 20*(3), 23–32.

ORITZ DE MONTELLANO, B. (1991). Multicultural pseudoscience: Spreading scientific illiteracy among minorities—Part 1. *Skeptical Inquirer, 16,* 46–50.

PAUL, R. (1993). *Critical thinking: What every person needs to know to survive in a rapidly changing world.* Santa Rosa, CA: Foundation for Critical Thinking.

PERKINS, D. (1992). *Smart schools: From training memories to educating minds.* New York: Free Press.

PERKINS, D. N., & SALOMON, G. (1987). Transfer and teaching thinking. In D. N. Perkins, J. Lochhead, & J. Bishop (Eds.), *Thinking: The second international conference* (pp. 285–303). Hillsdale, NJ: Erlbaum.

PERRY, R. P., ABRAMI, P. C., & LEVENTHAL, L. (1979). Educational seduction: The effect of instructor expressiveness and lecture content on student ratings and achievement. *Journal of Educational Psychology, 71*(1), 107–116.

PETTIT, P. (1993). Suspended judgment: Instituting a research ethic. *Controlled Clinical Trials, 14,* 261–265.

PHILLIPS, D. C. (1987). *Philosophy, science, and social inquiry: Contemporary methodological controversies in social science and related applied fields of research.* New York: Pergamon Press.

PHILLIPS, D. C. (1992). *A social scientist's bestiary: A guide to fabled, threats to, and defenses of, naturalistic social science.* New York: Pergamon Press.

PINTO, R. C., & BLAIR, J. A. (1993). *Reasoning: A practical guide.* Englewood Cliffs, NJ: Prentice-Hall.

POPPER, K. (1959). *The logic of scientific discovery.* London: Hutchinson.

POPPER, K. R. (1972). *Conjectures and refutations: The growth of scientific knowledge* (4th ed.). London: Routledge and Kegan Paul.

POPPER, K. (1992). *In search of a better world: Lectures and essays from thirty years.* New York: Routledge.

POPPER, K. R. (1994). M. A. Notturno (Ed.), *The myth of the framework: In defense of science and rationality.* New York: Routledge.

PRAWAT, R. S. (1989). Promoting access to knowledge, strategy, and disposition in students: A research synthesis. *Review of Educational Research, 59*(1), 1–41.

PRICE, J. L., & MANN, G. (1989, November). *Thinking skills and propaganda detection (ED315393).* Paper presented at the annual meeting of the Mid-South Educational Research Association, Little Rock, AR.

PSYCHOLOGICAL CORPORATION. (1980). *Watson-Glaser critical thinking appraisal.* San Diego, CA: Harcourt Brace Jovanovich.

RADNER, D., & RADNER, M. (1982). *Science and unreason.* Belmont, CA: Wadsworth.

RANK, H. (1982). *The pitch.* Park Forest, IL: Counter-Propaganda Press.

ROSAL, V. (1978). The nurse's role in the management of Parkinson's Disease. *The Journal of Nursing Care, 11*(2), 10, 12, 30.

RUGGERIO, V. R. (1984). *The art of thinking: A guide to critical and creative thought.* New York: Harper & Row.

SALOVEY, P., & TURK, D. C. (1988). Some effects of mood on clinicians' memory. In D. C. Turk & P. Salovey (Eds.), *Reasoning, inference and judgment in clinical psychology.* New York: Free Press.

SCALZI, C. C., BURKE, L. E., & GREENLAND, S. (1980). Evaluation of an inpatient educational program for coronary patients and families. *Heart and Lung, 9,* 846–853.

SCHEPER-HUGHES, N., & LOVELL, A. M. (1987). *Psychiatry inside out: Selected writings of Franco Basaglia.* New York: Columbia University Press.

SCHUERMAN, J. R. (1983). *Research and evaluation in the human services.* New York: Free Press.

SCHUSTACK, M. W., & STERNBERG, R. J. (1981). Evaluation of evidence in causal inference. *Journal of Experimental Psychology: General, 110*(1), 101–120.

SCHWARTZ, I. M. (1989). *(In)justice for juveniles: Rethinking the best interests of the child.* Lexington, MA: Heath.

SCHWARTZ, R. J., & PERKINS, D. N. (1990). *Teaching thinking: Issues and approaches.* Pacific Grove, CA: Critical Thinking Press & Software.

SCHWARTZ, S., & GRIFFIN, T. (1986). *Medical thinking: The psychology of medical judgment and decision making.* New York: Springer-Verlag.

SEECH, Z. (1993). *Open minds and everyday reasoning.* Belmont, CA: Wadsworth.

SHAFFER, D., VIELAND, V., GARLAND, A., ROJAS, M., UNDERWOOD, M., & BUSNER, C. (1990). Adolescent suicide attempters: Response to suicide prevention programs. *Journal of the American Medical Association, 264*(24), 3151–3155.

SIEGEL, D. H. (1993). Open adoptions of infants: Adoptive parent's perceptions of advantages. *Social Work, 38*(1), 15–23.

SILVERSTEIN, B. (1987). Toward a science of propaganda. *Political Psychology, 8*(1), 49–59.

SKRABANEK, P. (1990). Reductionist fallacies in the theory and treatment of mental disorders. *International Journal of Mental Health, 19*(3), 6–18.

SKRABANEK, P., & MCCORMICK, J. (1992). *Follies and fallacies in medicine* (2nd ed.). Chippenham, England: Tarragon Press.

SMITH, R. L. (1969). *At your own risk: The case against chiropractic.* New York: Pocket Books.

SNYDER, M., & WHITE, P. (1981). Testing hypotheses about other people: Strategies of verification and falsification. *Personality and Social Psychology Bulletin, 7*(1), 39–43.

Sox, H. C., Blatt, M. A., Higgins, M. C., & Marton, K. I. (1988). *Medical decision making.* Boston: Butterworth-Heinemann.

Stanovich, K. E. (1992). *How to think straight about psychology* (3rd ed.). New York: Harper Collins.

Stehl-Werner, J., & Gibbs, L. E. (1987). Clinicians' fallacies in psychiatric practice. *Journal of Psychosocial Nursing and Mental Health Services, 25*(8), 14–17.

Stepleton, S. S. (1989). The young child in group care. In E. A. Balcerzak (Ed.), *Group care of children: Transitions toward the year 2000* (pp. 255–270). Washington, DC: Child Welfare League of America.

Stewart, C. J., & Cash, W. B. (1982). *Interviewing: Principles and practice.* Dubuque, IA: Wm. C. Brown.

Streissguth, A. P., Barr, H. M., Sampson, P. D., Darby, B. L., & Martin, D. C. (1989). IQ at age 4 in relation to maternal alcohol use and smoking during pregnancy. *Developmental Psychology, 25*(1), 3–11.

Szasz, T. (1994). *Cruel compassion: Psychiatric control of society's unwanted.* New York: Wiley.

Tallant, N. (1988). *Psychological report writing* (3rd ed.). Englewood Cliffs, NJ: Prentice Hall.

Tanner, C. A. (1987). Teaching clinical judgment. *Annual Review of Nursing Research, 5,* 153–173.

Tavris, C. (1992). *The mismeasure of women.* New York: Simon & Schuster.

Tavris, C. (1994). The illusion of science in psychiatry. *Skeptic, 2*(3), 78–85.

Thayer-Bacon, B. J. (1993). Caring and its relationship to critical thinking. *Educational Theory, 43*(3), 323–340.

Thelen, T. (1993). *Critical thinking and cumulative grade point average correlations of senior baccalaureate nursing students.* Unpublished Master of Science in Nursing Thesis, University of Wisconsin—Eau Claire, Eau Claire, WI.

Thouless, R. H. (1974). *Straight and crooked thinking: Thirty-eight dishonest tricks of debate.* London: Pan.

Tversky, A., & Kahneman, D. (1973). Availability: A heuristic for judging frequency and probability. *Cognitive Psychology, 5,* 207–232.

Tversky, A., & Kahneman, D. (1974). Judgment under uncertainty: Heuristics and biases. *Science, 185,* 1124–1131.

Tversky, A., & Kahneman, D. (1982). Judgment under uncertainty: Heuristics and biases. In D. Kahneman, P. Slovic, & A. Tversky (Eds.). *Judgment under uncertainty: Heuristics and biases.* Cambridge: Cambridge University Press.

Von Winterfeldt, D., & Edwards, W. (1986). *Decision analysis and behavioral research.* Cambridge, England: Cambridge University Press.

Vosniadou, S., & Ortony, A. (1989). Similarity and analogical reasoning: A synthesis. In S. Vosniadou & A. Ortony (Eds.), *Similarity and analogical reasoning* (pp. 1–17). Cambridge, England: Cambridge University Press.

Voss, J. F. (1987). Learning and transfer in subject-matter learning: A problem-solving model. *International Journal of Educational Research, 11,* 607–622.

Ware, J. E., & Williams, R. G. (1975). The Dr. Fox effect: A study of lecturer effectiveness and ratings of instruction. *Journal of Medical Education, 50,* 149–156.

WATSON, G., & GLASER, E. M. (1980). *Watson-Glaser Critical Thinking Appraisal.* Cleveland, OH: The Psychological Corporation.

WEBER, K., FRANKENBERGER, W., & HEILMAN, K. (1992). The effects of methylphenidate on the academic achievement of children diagnosed with attention-deficit hyperactivity disorder. *Developmental Disabilities Bulletin, 20,* 49–68.

WEDDLE, P. (1978). *Argument: A guide to critical thinking.* New York: McGraw-Hill.

WEINSTEIN, M. C., FINEBERG, H. V., ELSTEIN, A. S., FRAZIER, H. S., NEUHAUSER, D., NEUTRA, R. R., & MCNEIL, B. J. (1980). *Clinical decision analysis.* Philadelphia: Saunders.

WEISBERG, R. (1986). *Creativity, genius and other myths.* New York: W. H. Freeman.

WEIST, M. D., FINNEY, J. W., & OLLENDICK, T. H. (1992). Cognitive biases in child behavior therapy. *The Behavior Therapist, 15*(10), 249–252.

WELLBUTRIN (1992). WELLBUTRIN (bupropion HCL), the non-serotonergic alternative to Prozac (fluoxetine HCL) for many patients. *American Journal of Psychiatry, 149*(5), A33–A37.

WESTON, A. (1992). *A rulebook for arguments.* (2nd ed.). Indianapolis, IN: Hackett.

WEXLER, R. (1990). *Wounded innocents: The real victims of the war against child abuse.* Buffalo, NY: Prometheus Press.

WHITTINGTON, C. (1986). Literature review: Transfer of learning in social work education. *British Journal of Social Work, 16,* 571–577.

WILLIAMS, R. G., & WARE, J. E. (1976). Validity of student ratings of instruction under different incentive conditions: A further study of the Dr. Fox effect. *Journal of Educational Psychology, 68*(1), 48–56.

WOOD, G. (1978). The knew-it-all-along effect. *Journal of Experimental Psychology, Human Perception and Performance, 4,* 345–353.

YARKIN, K. L., TOWN, J. P., & HARVEY, J. H. (1981). The role of cognitive sets in interpreting and remembering interpersonal events. In J. H. Harvey (Ed.), *Cognition, social behavior, and the environment* (pp. 289–308). Hillsdale, NJ: Lawrence Erlbaum Associates.

YOUNG, J. H. (1992). *American health quackery.* Princeton, NJ: Princeton University Press.

ZINGG, R. M. (1941). India's wolf children. *Scientific American, 164*(3), 135–137.

ZUNG, W. W. K. (1965). A self-rating depression scale. *Archives of General Psychiatry, 12,* 63–70.

INDEX

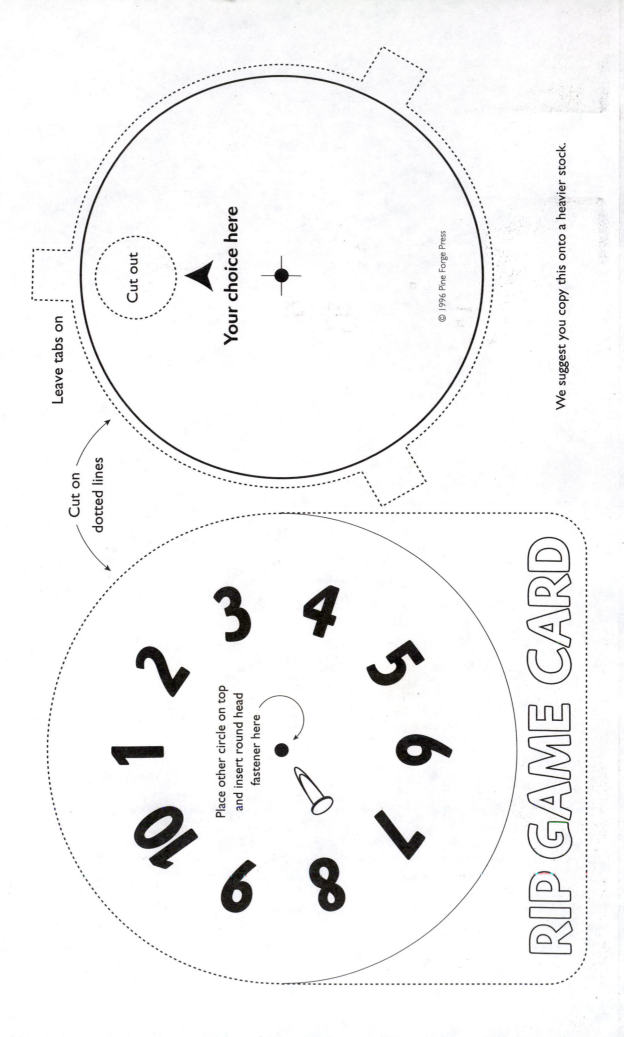

Cut out

Your choice here

© 1996 Pine Forge Press

Leave tabs on

Cut on
dotted lines

We suggest you copy this onto a heavier stock.

2 3 4
1   5
10   6
  9 8 7

Place other circle on top
and insert round head
fastener here

RIP GAME CARD